I0435409

My Fight for Humanity: Advocating for Justice, Equality, and Human Dignity

Gabriel Filer

CreateSpace Independent Publishing Platform

CONTENTS

FOREWORD
CHARDON MURRAY

When I first met Gabriel Filer, he was a quiet but ambitious young man who was compelled to call legislators in North Carolina to encourage them to open their hearts and minds. Gabe told me that he was from Connecticut, and thankful that they had legalized gay marriage, but that he wanted to be more involved nationally. I was very impressed by his passion and commitment, and his interest in SB 526, the School Bullying Bill that my legislator had championed to try and positively impact the lives of gay youth.

Research tells us that LGBT youth are 4 times more likely to attempt suicide when compared to their straight peers. Research also tells us, definitively, that bullying has an impact: self-harm increases by 2.5 times with each bullying incident.

As I listened to Gabe recount his life story, the story that he will share with you in this book, I was brought to tears. Gabe had endured hardships which would have snuffed out the hope of any average person. Gabe had been a statistic: he had attempted to take his own life. However, he was determined that this would not be the end of his story. He has chosen to take his own experiences and convert that pain, heartache, and negativity into a drive to positively impact others.

Gabe and I have remained in touch over the years, and I'm always pleased to get updates from him about what he has accomplished. It amazes me that this talented, passionate, and confident young man is the same quiet person I spoke to over the phone so many years ago.

Gabe is not a statistic. He has proven that good can come out of bad experiences, as he continues to work hard to improve the lives of others who are suffering as he once did.

Chardon Murray, M.A.
Professor of Criminology and Sociology
Cape Fear Community College
Wilmington, NC

AUTHOR'S NOTE

I initially began this project when I was twenty-one years old. Since the Washington legislature passed same-sex marriage, I realized that a landmark decision from the Connecticut Supreme Court would someday transform into a national issue.

During my junior year of college, I told a very trusted co-worker that I started a book entitled *My Fight for Humanity: Advocating for Justice, Equality, and Human Dignity*. In February 2012 I met with a faculty member at the University of Washington to discuss my options to publish a book, which detailed my experience advocating for human rights. During our meeting, this individual expressed serious doubt that I would be able to publish my work through a university, however she encouraged me to explore opportunities in self-publishing. Despite the fact I developed a very lengthy manuscript, I ultimately decided to table this project for nearly three years.

A month before I graduated from the University of Washington, I met a young author named Jake Ducey. In April 2013 Jake published his first book (which covered his six-month journey around the world). While he wrote this book he expressed that he never secured an immediate publishing deal. He also explained that it's very common for authors to finish writing a book even before they find a publisher. His remarks were highly instrumental when it came to acknowledging that I could someday share my own story.

In August 2014 I began pursuing a Master of City and Regional Planning at The Ohio State University. Moving to Ohio was an extremely difficult decision given the state's conservative history. For several months, I felt really uncomfortable residing in the state that gave President Bush the keys to a second term. What I found more distasteful was learning how hostile Ohio's state government was towards the LGBT community. Ohio is one of only three states which refuses to issue a new (or modified) birth certificate to any individual who undergoes a sex reassignment surgery.

When I first started graduate school, I tried my best to reverse numerous inequities through the legislative process. My attempts to advance a comprehensive anti-bullying law was never met with success once the Chair of the House Judiciary committee voiced his opposition to protecting LGBT students in public schools. I was appalled that *one* person could prevent crucial legislation from even being debated. Being in the minority meant my voice was practically nonexistent in state government.

On November 6, 2014 the United States Court of Appeals for the Sixth Circuit upheld same-sex marriage bans in four states (including Ohio). Two days later, I resumed writing my first book because I not only intend to use this opportunity to share my eight-year journey in politics, but I'm going to stress *your* voice truly matters.

Disclaimer: Although I cover human rights extensively in this book, my focus pertains to this issue as it relates to women and the LGBT community. This book does not cover human rights pertaining to children, asylum seekers, and indigenous populations.

INTRODUCTION

I never envisioned pursuing a career in politics. Shortly after the Connecticut Supreme Court issued a landmark ruling paving the way for same-sex marriage, I heard an urgent call to go forth into the world and help others. When I was seventeen years old I fought back against attempts to outlaw same-sex marriage in the Connecticut Constitution. Despite the fact I was unable to vote, I used each day as an opportunity to advance the rights of gays and lesbians.

Once Connecticut legalized same-sex marriage I turned my attention to bigger challenges within the gay rights movement. Within a month, I contacted over sixty state lawmakers and organizations in seven states and began advocating for gay rights nationwide. During lunch breaks and study halls, I used my guidance counselor's office as a phone banking center. When I was seventeen years old I acquired a unique role in the gay rights movement. I was one of only a few individuals who were fortunate to reside in a state that recognized same-sex marriage in 2008.

During my senior year of high school, I found myself playing political offense because I was determined to advance the values of my home state across America. In 2009, I teamed with North Carolina State Senator Julia Boseman to help advance the School Violence Prevention Act. This provision protected LGBT students from being bullied in public schools. During the legislative session, I testified and organized efforts to advance a controversial gay rights bill through a conservative legislature. Two days before I graduated high school, the School Violence Prevention Act passed by one vote. North Carolina became the ninth state to enact a comprehensive anti-bullying law. Since then, ten states have reexamined the way they address school violence.

After breaking a forty-year legislative impasse and averting a Constitutional Convention, I thought my career in politics finally ended. Towards the end of 2011 Katy Buck, the Legislative Aide for Washington State Representative Jamie Pedersen approached me shortly before Christmas. She informed me that Democrats were preparing to introduce legislation which legalized same-sex marriage. Just before my twenty-first birthday I heard another unexpected call to go forth and help others. Three years after campaigning for same-sex marriage in Connecticut, I strategized another legislative plan to make history. This time around I was working to propel same-sex marriage in the first western state. Throughout this campaign cycle, I teamed with friends to help launch grassroots fundraising efforts. In addition, I delivered many powerful speeches regarding human rights on my college campus.

On November 6, 2012 Washington, Maine, and Maryland made history by approving same-sex marriage via referendum. This victory ensured this issue would someday be sent to the United States Supreme Court.

Shortly after campaigning for same-sex marriage on both coasts, I decided to focus on international law and human rights abroad. During my final year of college I launched a human rights blog. My objective was to cover upcoming elections in Australia and South Africa. In addition, I reached out to Nelson Mandela two days before I graduated college. I thanked President Mandela for championing the first Constitution protecting gays and lesbians from discrimination. I also thanked the former South African President for vowing to affirm human dignity remains a constitutional right.

Once I finished college I thought my job was truly finished. Five years after I shepherd the School Violence Prevention Act, I was awakened to another call to go forth and help others. On August 20, 2014 I began breaking another glass ceiling. My objective was to advocate for a comprehensive anti-bullying law in Ohio. Throughout graduate school, I continued my legislative efforts to expand the rights of gays and lesbians. During this time I remained politically active because the LGBT community is subject to numerous injustices. As I pursue my graduate studies, I will continue advancing the interests of the LGBT community during this critical moment because this is the civil rights issue of my generation. This book captures my eight-year political journey which eventually led to the United States Supreme Court.

1 OVERCOMING AUTISM

"After climbing a great hill, one only finds that there are many more hills to climb."
-Nelson Mandela

I was born a fighter. A few days after my third birthday my parents received news from a clinical psychologist that I was diagnosed with autism. I was diagnosed with Pervasive Development Disorder, a learning disability on the autism spectrum by Dr. Michael Powers. Throughout my first three years I was unable to read, write, or compile a sentence. Many parents and physicians agree that the first three years of a child's life is the most critical stage of brain development. During infancy, the brain undergoes a significant period of growth. My parents decided to take action because they believed my school district was depriving me from receiving an adequate education.

Throughout my childhood, I relied on a supportive team of mentors, lawyers, medical experts, and family members. This group of people played a very instrumental role to helping me overcome my learning disability. College students (from Wesleyan University) would visit my house on a daily basis. Many tutors spent several hours teaching me a variety of learning activities one-on-one. Most of these tutorial sessions were highly intensive and individualized to meet my capabilities. Learning in a home environment allowed me to thrive academically because I was in close proximity to family and it sheltered me from any malign systems of thought. Learning in this setting allowed me to personalize and create a harmonious learning space.

During summer break most children my age played outside and participated in fun outdoor activities, however I spent numerous vacations pushing myself towards recovery. During the school year I was required to complete a dozen academic workbooks (on top of my regular school assignments). My study area was either a triangular birch table or my Little Tikes elephant slide (both of which were located in my basement).

Whenever I wanted to work in privacy I tucked myself beneath my blue elephant slide and used that space to focus on assignments. I remember one afternoon (when I was seven years old) in late July when I managed to successfully complete ten workbooks in one sitting. I used my elephant slide to read through several stories and circle which answer best matched each question. I also identified if a situation was true, false, or inferred based on the content of each narrative. Although this work was tedious, I rarely questioned my tutor's method of instruction.

Aside from attending tutorial sessions and elementary school, I had to visit an occupational therapist and speech pathologist each week. I met with Jeanne Kagan, an occupational therapist who worked at Connecticut Children's Medical Center. During my sessions with Jeanne, she assigned me to tasks, which were designed to enhance my motor skills. For instance, she frequently timed how fast I could run from one end of a hallway to another. In addition, she tested my ability to walk across a narrow balance beam. She even challenged me to draw two circles simultaneously on a white board using both hands.

In addition to visiting an occupational therapist, I also met (on a weekly basis) with Karen Anthony, a speech pathologist who specializes in communication disorders. Her activities focused on improving my cognitive, verbal, and communication skills. During my sessions with her (which lasted between 1-2 hours) she would teach me vocabulary and ask me to compile a sentence using a random set of words. She introduced me to analogies, synonyms, and antonyms. The most appealing aspect of her work was that it occurred in a home setting (which reminded me of my tutorial sessions). Throughout the months of November and December her house was furnished with Holiday decorations. Each year she assembled a giant Christmas tree in her living room. Her Christmas tree was equipped with white lights and was neatly ornamented with small candy canes. Karen went to great lengths to ensure her house was presentable. As a child, it was easy for me to adapt to her learning environment because she removed any potential distractions and outside people. Intense sessions of one-on-one academic support became a vital ingredient of my recovery.

On November 22, 2000 Dr. Michael Powers (the same clinical psychologist who initially diagnosed me) lifted my diagnosis of Pervasive Development Disorder when I was nine years old. After undergoing an intensive Neuropsychological Evaluation, my parents were informed I no longer met the criteria for my learning disability. During that time, my condition became more consistent with a diagnosis of Attention Deficit Hyperactivity Disorder (ADHD).

Dr. Powers noted in his report; "Gabriel was quite engaging and his language skills improved dramatically. Eye contact was good. He was entirely cooperative throughout the evaluation. His physical examination was unremarkable...It is Dr. Powers' opinion that Gabriel more likely fulfills criteria for Attention Deficit Hyperactivity Disorder." My parents were gratified once they received this news. My mother choked back tears and my father beamed with happiness. During this final meeting, they left his office knowing how much their hard work paid off.

Secret Strength: Three Stages of Introverted Sensing

Although I overcame Pervasive Development Disorder, I experience something most people with autism never face. Introverted sensing and object perception both collect data in the present moment and compare it with past experience. This process evokes the feelings associated with memory. The most concrete definition I can offer is imagine meeting someone you knew from your past. This person could be dead or alive. Imagine being given a second chance to introduce yourself to a special person. As I meet new people in life, my learning disability has allowed me to relive past friendships. Living with this unique strength is truly a blessing because it helps me not only heal distant relationships, but it reaffirms the importance of embracing harmonious friendships.

The three most important stages of human object perception include: identifying, connecting, and, sharing. The first stage of object perception is often the most common because it involves the least amount of mental and emotional output. Whenever I meet someone I first ask myself, "Does this person look like somebody from my past?" If the person does not look familiar, my brain will treat this conversation as a typical experience. However, if I come across a person whose physical appearance replicates someone I know—I will immediately recognize certain characteristics.

On one occasion this got me into a lot of trouble. In March 2014 I attended a graduate Open House. During this event I came across a guy named Devin. He was a first-year graduate student who carried a distinct physical appearance. Despite being only twenty-three years old, he resembled somebody much older. Devin was tall and well toned. He enjoyed exercising. Before heading to the gym he always wears a form-fitting t-shirt and tight sweatpants. Devin enjoys purchasing the latest designer clothes and glasses. He combs his dark brown hair to the side and sports a sharp appearance before he leaves his house each morning. Devin grooms himself as if he is about to step on stage. This man is truly a promoter—he swings deals unlike any individual. I usually maintain a healthy distance from people who exhibit his personality because they are eager to start drama.

Five months after I first encountered Devin at Open House, I was shopping with my father for groceries at Wal-Mart. While I pushed my cart down the isle I saw a man whose dark facial hair, blue eyes, and glasses resemble the student I met at Open House. This tall man wore tight sweatpants and a Chicago football cap. As he was pushing a young toddler in his cart, I figured that Devin must be a father. I didn't feel comfortable directly approaching this person because I figured that I would see him in just a few days.

During my graduate orientation I approached Devin at a bar and asked him if he has a son. In a completely *vexed* face this individual slowly walked towards me (in utter silence). Little did I know he was just about to start a scene—the first words from this angry drunk were:

> *"Can you help me pay this month's child support so I don't get thrown in jail again? Who do you think I am? I never shop at Wal-Mart! I'll never purchase my fuckin' son anything from there..."*

As soon as this spewing volcanic mouthpiece receded, I was

speechless. I never envisioned that my experience in human object perception would ever result in a five-minute lecture over child support. Instead of receiving a simple up or down answer—I was subject to hearing a vile service announcement from an intoxicated twenty-three-year-old. Although the first stage of human object perception is the most practical, it often entails the most errors because my mind formulates a decision solely on physical appearance.

The second stage of object perception involves connecting both personal and physical traits between two individuals. Both individuals in the second stage of object perception could be living or dead. This phase usually requires a bit more mental and emotional effort. Unlike the first phase, which typically entails looking at someone's physical appearance, I have to formulate a personal connection with someone (which sometimes includes a complete stranger) and bridge that information with someone from my past. The second phase requires additional time because whenever I meet a new person I not only have to detect physical similarities, but I need to understand if they share any common interests.

On August 26, 2014 I unexpectedly crossed paths with someone familiar. As I walked by myself during this quiet afternoon I quickly glanced inside a vacant classroom. I saw a student sitting alone reading a large book. I slowly walked towards this familiar face and struck up a casual conversation. Although I never met this person, he reminded me of someone from my family.

His name was Alex Wesaw; he was a slightly tall and slender twenty-four-year-old pursuing his PhD in City and Regional Planning. The two most distinct features about this individual were his eyes and blonde hair. During my conversation I asked, "What is your ethnic background?" Although many people might find this question distasteful, I could not ignore how much he mirrored my father's oldest brother Christ Filer. His appearance resembled my uncle so much that I thought we were mysteriously related. Alex wore glasses and side-combed his blonde hair just like my uncle when he was young.

Before I notified Alex how much he resembles Christ Filer, I did my best to form a strong relationship. Throughout the semester, I used several forms of indirect communication to briefly introduce my uncle over a long period of time. I spent several hours strategizing how I was going to connect a twenty-four-year-old graduate student to a sixty-six-year-old grandfather from Massachusetts. Before I decided to reach out to Alex I carefully deliberated *how* I was going to inform him about my family.

In late September I composed a lengthy e-mail detailing my personal connections to Boston. In this letter, I used keywords such as Elizabeth Warren, Boston Red Sox, and Boston Public Garden to help Alex learn more about the area. I also sent him the link to my cousin's online jewelry store.

Before I formally notify any individual about a secret relationship—I do my best to understand if they would share any common interests. During my first semester, I asked Alex if he excelled in chemistry. Alex told me, *"I received an A in high school Chemistry."* As soon as I heard his response I realized his interests were well in line with my uncle.

Since I started graduate school, I deliberated for several weeks. I wanted to determine when it was most appropriate to reveal that Alex looks just like my uncle. As weeks passed, it marked another missed opportunity. Every time I witnessed Alex lock his office door, it reinforced the fact I needed to face my fear. Throughout the semester I was *terrified* to approach this student because I didn't want to experience another embarrassing episode. Alex intimated me because he was reserved. His lack of expressiveness made it difficult for me to acquire the comfort to readily approach him.

On the day before Thanksgiving break, I *finally* faced my fear. November 20, 2014 marked the day I broke my silence. Just before Alex left his office—I timidly pulled him aside and asked if we could both talk privately. My stomach *churned* vociferously because I was gambling another relationship. I told myself, "If I *ever* screwed up...I would *live* with this for the rest of my graduate career." As soon as I approached this student, he walked me to a secluded area within the School of Architecture. As I sat next to him on an antique bench—I revealed my deepest thoughts. In a *shallow* voice, I softly muttered:

> "You look *just like* my uncle. *Your* appearance is *very* similar to what he looked like forty years ago. When I look at you—I see my father's oldest brother when he was in his twenties. I find it *ironic* that two people who have never met share countless similarities..."

As I looked straight ahead I was *smacked* with a powerful presence of light. My face was overwhelmed by this body of energy. During the end of this intense conversation I struggled to maintain appropriate eye contact. I did my best to consciously ignore the guilt and pain I felt inside. Opening up about this experience was incredibly difficult because I had not seen my uncle in over five years. During that afternoon someone was watching over me, once I felt this individual's presence my emotions were ready to succumb.

It was too painful for me to reveal too much family history. Holding a straight face was unimaginably strenuous because I was speaking to my uncle. This moment was completely surreal because my brain flashed back to when I was in high school. Within a few minutes, I recalled several past memories of my grandfather.

My Grandfather: A Remarkable Legacy

My grandfather Charles Filer is an inspiring individual. He spent most of his career serving in the military. His career in the military started before World War II with the United States Army Air Corps at Bradley Airfield. During World War II he served the 57th Fighter Group in the 65th Squadron. This mission included campaigns in North Africa and Italy. He was recognized with a Bronze Medal of Honor for his remarkable service in the Mediterranean Theatre and for his heroism when he went beyond the call of duty for attempting to save the life of a pilot. A defining moment during his tenure was when he was promoted to the rank of Captain in the United States Air Force.

Upon returning to civilian life, Charles Filer worked as an aircraft mechanist at Pratt & Whitney. Later in his career he spent several years working at his local post office. My grandfather spent his final years in a small town outside Toledo, Ohio. During my childhood I would make frequent road trips with my family to visit his house. His first wife died when my father was twenty-two years old. My grandfather was the glue of the family because he had to step up during tough times.

Charles made extraordinary sacrifices because he believed in the potential of others around him. Each year he would mail me a birthday card (which included a kind note and $20). Despite living on a fixed-income, he was remarkably generous. His generosity and loyalty frequently involved him giving up his evenings and weekends to help with building projects and house remodeling.

One afternoon my grandfather was doing work on his roof, he fell off his ladder and almost died. He was rushed to the hospital and doctors determined that he damaged several organs. Since that accident his health was never the same. During my freshman year of high school my family relocated him to Connecticut. There was no question my father felt most comfortable taking care of Charles, however I believe he didn't want Charles to stay at our house because he didn't want me to carry the emotional burden of seeing someone's health decline.

During my sophomore year of high school my grandfather was placed in a rehabilitation center (I was never told that it was hospice). Whether consciously or unconsciously I tried to ignore that his final months were fast approaching. I sparingly met with him because I did not have the strength of emotion to watch someone suffer.

In April 2007 Charles was transferred to Hartford Hospital. One Saturday afternoon my father approached me and told me that he wanted to visit Charles. When I asked my father *why* he wanted me to see him, he casually said, "life's a bit short and you want to capture every moment...*come on* let's go and see him one more time."

My dad's response was very brief; he seemed reluctant to volunteer any information. I had little knowledge of my grandfather's condition because I hadn't seen him in several months.

Whenever I do not see someone for an extended period—it's easy to believe his or her reality is frozen in time. The last moment I saw Charles was at my aunt's house in 2006. During that evening he was fine. I remember engaging in casual conversations and hearing him strike up the latest jokes with my aunt.

On April 21, 2007 I traveled with my father to Hartford Hospital. With the exception of my occupational therapy sessions, I never spent much of my childhood in hospitals. Once we entered the main lobby my father asked a receptionist which room Charles was treated. My father and I traveled up two sets of elevators to the eleventh floor. Once I stepped outside my innocence was altered.

After not seeing my grandfather in several months—I couldn't *recognize* him. I held back tears and just remained quite for several moments. I was *speechless* because I never encountered anyone who I could not physically recognize. My remarkable strengths in object perception and introverted sensing were not enough for me to identify the stranger sitting in front of me.

Charles could barley open his eyes or speak; his nostrils were connected to an oxygen mask. I was silent because I could tell he was in a lot of pain. I did not have the emotional maturity to find anything fulfilling about this experience. I only saw what was right in front of me and that was watching someone deteriorate.

The worst part about visiting my grandfather was that I thought he was a stranger. I could not believe I was related to the person in front of me. His physical appearance did not resemble the person I met at Cedar Point when I was still a toddler, the man who spent each evening watching *Jeopardy*, or the generous relative who paid for countless dinners.

On the evening of April 25, 2007 my mother asked me if I wanted to see Charles Filer at the hospital one last time. She told me in a shockingly calm manner that he would not likely make it past tonight. After deliberating for roughly an hour I decided to stay home. I followed my gut by not visiting my grandfather during his final day. I do not regret this decision because too many people were in that room. I did not feel that it was healthy to witness a person's body undergo the most unimaginable stages of physical decay. At the end of the day, I wanted his spirit and body to be restored to time he never felt any pain.

On April 26, 2007 I woke up as if it were a normal day. My lunch was already packed and my calendar was booked with events. Once I went downstairs my mother told me, "Your grandfather passed away five hours ago."

At first, I showed no emotion. I did my best to put on a brave face. When I was a teenager my brain was not fully developed. As a result, it took me longer periods of time to digest the complexity of many situations.

As I finished breakfast I saw a television commercial for the hospital where my grandfather died. Towards the end of the commercial I ran upstairs and locked myself in my room. I sat on my bed because I realized he was gone. For the next ten minutes I released several months of pain I was forced to repress. Although Charles Filer lived a long life, his final months were too painful to witness. It was extremely cruel to watch someone's decline stretch for an eternity. The only hope I felt that day was that he was in a better place and that I might see him again someday.

When I was sixteen years old I could not understand the depth or complexity of my grandfather's death. I never imagined this day would ever come back and hit me in the face when I was least prepared. During my junior year of college I would relive my grandfather's final moments. This was not the last time I saw him.

2 GOING SOMEWHERE

"I don't have any skeletons in my closet that can't be allowed out."
-Walter Isaacson

I grew up being an ugly duckling. Since the fifth grade I was frequently bullied. I wasn't too interested in dating because I never found myself attracted to anyone. Between seventh and eighth grade my life was in limbo. I began to question my sexuality because I was attracted to both men and women. At this time, I wasn't sure which gender I favored because I viewed love and sex as separate entities.

On February 10, 2005 I stepped inside my high school for the very first time. I was smacked with an undeniable truth. One immediate distinction between myself and others was the fact most students finished puberty. The male students at my high school were not only taller, but their bodies boasted jaw-dropping curves. As I walked across the hallway I felt intimidated.

Before I knew it, I was shaking hands with the star of my high school football team. As I glanced at this Sicilian beefcake my stomach fell to the ground. His crystal blue eyes immediately grabbed my attention. This teenager's appearance reinforced masculine stereotypes. His scalp was saturated with hair gel and large swaths of muscle covered each part of his body.

As I walked away my face suddenly turned bright pink because it marked the first time I felt infatuated. My first impression of this student transformed the way I view human relationships. At first, I wasn't sure if February 10, 2005 was an isolated event or if it marked the moment I recognized my sexual identity. During the next several months I deliberated whether or not I was really gay. At this time I asked myself, "What causes me to experience infatuation? What elements in humans do I find most physically attractive?" Once I witnessed the physical transformation men undergo after puberty I determined that I wanted to pursue a same-sex relationship.

As joyful as I thought it would be to have a male partner, I found it difficult to reconcile a romantic and idealized concept of conjugal life. I was a bit anxious about entering a same-sex relationship because I wondered who would perform yard work, cook dinner, or clean the bathrooms. On one occasion, I asked myself, "How do same-sex couples delegate household tasks?"

I initially feared living an alternative lifestyle because I knew I would immediately be stamped as "too effeminate" and "thin-skinned." Another reason I was hesitant to declare my sexual identity was the fact I feared subsequent repercussions. Being a gay youth would open up the floodgates to perpetual harassment and social rejection. When I was fourteen years old, I didn't feel it was appropriate to confront my sexuality because I feared how others would judge me.

One person I trusted was Cheryl (my paraprofessional). I first met her when I was eleven years old. Even though I made significant progress overcoming my learning disability, my parents insisted that I continue to receive academic assistance from a paraprofessional. Since I did not have many friends I used Cheryl as a mentor to help me survive each school day.

My relationship with her grew over the years because I would report directly to her if I experienced any bullying incidents or needed help completing school assignments. Aside from assisting me with daily activities, Cheryl and I would frequently enjoy long conversations pertaining to issues such as the environment, cooking, and travel. My family would send Christmas cookies to her house each year because they wanted to thank her for incredible support.

While I was coming to terms with my sexual orientation, I began to follow current events. On April 21, 2005 I listened to National Public Radio (NPR) on my way to school. During the morning headlines, a female voice on the radio announced:

"Connecticut joins Vermont to become the second state to permit civil unions. Yesterday the Connecticut State Senate approved civil unions by a vote of 27-9. Six Republicans joined Senate Democrats to help pass this measure. Republican Governor Jodi Rell, a supporter of civil unions signed the bill into law."

I walked into school with a smile on my face. Despite being bullied on a regular basis, I realized someone believed in the welfare of gays and lesbians. When I was fourteen years old there were very few people I could celebrate this precious moment with. I decided to share this news with my paraprofessional because I built a strong connection with her. Before first period, Cheryl and I sat at a corner table located in the back of Algebra class. Ten minutes before first period she arrived with her McDonald's coffee. When I first saw her I was overjoyed to share what I recently learned.

Since my paraprofessional never mentioned politics I figured it was safe to discuss gay rights. As soon as she sat down, I asked; "What do you think about Connecticut legalizing civil unions?" At first her face showed no emotion. Seconds later, Cheryl looked at me in the eye and said she wanted to move to another state. Her presence quickly *ignited* with hatred. She was not only enraged by the margin of legislative support, but she was more upset a Republican Governor signed it into law. My paraprofessional started referring to Connecticut as being a *"sore-thumb."* As malicious comments poured out of her mouth, I felt rattled.

During the next several weeks, her attacks against gays and lesbians continued. She used several fear tactics to scare me away from pursuing a same-sex relationship. One afternoon she expressed, *"gay children should be put up for adoption!"*

A few days later, she started talking about HIV/AIDS. My paraprofessional suggested that I could someday contract the HIV virus. She described in graphic detail two ways gay men contract HIV/AIDS. During this conversation, she grabbed her pen and used her arm to mimic how gay men share needles. She credits her experience working as a medical assistant to justify how gay men are more susceptible to contracting sexually transmitted diseases.

My body aversely reacted to her graphic lectures. I realized my days with her were numbered. I knew from that point it was not a matter of *if* our friendship would end; it was just a matter of *when.* It sickened me that someone I trust would interpret my sexual orientation as a disease. If being gay cost me a three-year friendship, I wondered what I would lose next.

The turmoil between Cheryl and I mutually caused both of us to silently withdraw as a way of setting limits rather than express our wounded feelings. Growing up with autism, it's really difficult for me to identify indirect social cues. Nevertheless, it's extremely devastating when someone leaves your life without providing any formal notice. My fourteen-year-old brain wasn't completely developed and it's difficult to detect whenever an individual misrepresents the truth. Even though my paraprofessional mailed a cheerful card after I finished middle school, I knew deep inside she wasn't being genuine.

Cheryl was well aware of my sexual orientation months before I "came out." The most painful part of this experience was the fact she resorted to fear tactics in order to prevent me from being myself. She claimed that loving another man would result in HIV. At the same time, she appealed to my own family by sending cards. Her actions left me deeply confused and upset because I saw two sides of her personality unfold simultaneously.

By June 2005 I came to terms with my sexual orientation. I didn't feel comfortable conforming to someone else's values. Even if I made enemies, it was best to remain authentic. In the months after I finished middle school, I never heard from Cheryl. Although she was not involved in my everyday life, I would face her wrath again. Three years after our friendship ended, gay rights would resurface for statewide discussion. Just when I was ready for closure, I found myself embattled in yet another unexpected fight.

High School: Not Exactly World Peace

My freshman year of high school was a really difficult experience because the bullying I encountered began to escalate. On one occasion a football player pretended to be my boyfriend. In September 2005, a seventeen-year-old football player approached me during lunch. His first words were, *"What up Gabe!"* In a completely puzzled face I said, "I'm alright." I didn't know this individual and I was initially skeptical of his intentions. When I encountered this athlete I thought he was too good to be true. I asked myself, "Why would a football player at my high school have any interest in me?" Although I was not initially attracted to him, my feelings about this person changed once he informed me he was gay. During my freshman year he flirted with me by saying comments like, *"You're handsome"* and *"I love you."* My close friend Rachel Margolis developed an ominous feeling he was being deceitful. She pleaded me to stay away from him. One afternoon I stayed after school to finish a Spanish quiz, as I left my teacher's classroom I saw this athlete kissing another woman whose body was thrusted against the locker. My stomach fell to the ground as I filled with envy and disgust. I turned my face away, however he and his girlfriend followed me down the hall. They continued to make out in the most vile and repulsive manner until I left the building.

Students at my high school are allocated a twenty-minute lunch period. Although I enrolled in honor classes, I was assigned the same lunch wave as most student athletes. Many athletes at my high school enrolled in basic level courses to avoid academic probation. As a result, my lunch wave combined freshmen (enrolled in honor classes) and juniors (enrolled in basic classes). November 3, 2005 was the day I hit rock bottom. During lunch, a girl stole my food. This student took my lunch because she wanted me to inform the entire lunch table (which had about 12 students) something about my sexual orientation.

When I refused to cooperate she called an older student athlete to the table and they would say something derogatory to my face. The first person who came to my lunch table was the captain of the girl's soccer team. This student started a fifteen-minute session of personal attacks. In a jocular manner she exclaimed, *"I'm really sorry if you don't have any friends...that's not my problem!"* After she left the table the student who held my lunch called the captain of the boy's soccer team. This individual was never kind to me. Earlier in the year, this athlete disseminated rumors that my genitals were small.

Once he arrived at the table I knew it was going to be ugly. He came within close contact and used intimidation techniques to coerce me to reveal extremely sensitive information. At first he shouted sexually vile remarks. Since I was silent, the girl who stole my lunch provided false statements, which provoked the soccer captain to direct his animosity towards me. In a loud voice he screamed, *"fuck you"* in front of my entire lunch table. Everyone laughed and not one person said a word in my defense.

Despite this hostility, I paid little attention to the other students. During the final three minutes I was silent. I did my best to think about my future. What gave me the strength of emotion to survive those fifteen minutes was hope. Throughout this incident, I looked outside a nearby window and thought to myself, "Someday I will move far away...in five years these people won't even matter."

The thought of living in another city kept my emotions stable (for the time being). Once lunch was over I walked to class by myself. I never felt so isolated in my life. During the second half of English class I was shaken. My English teacher noticed I was shockingly quiet. Thirty-five minutes later in Geometry class I broke down in tears. I finally succumbed to a violent storm of hate. After enduring a fifteen-minute session of personal attacks from both the captain(s) of the football and soccer team I decided to report their behavior to school officials. After lunch I went to the Vice Principal's office and wrote a detailed report describing my most painful experience in high school.

Once I decided to report this incident to school officials, I would have to own that decision and take heat from many colleagues in years to come. I was determined to put my welfare ahead of a group of sophomoric loony toons that never cared about my existence. From the moment I reported this incident—there was no looking back.

Shortly after I documented the bullying incident to the Vice Principal, the captain(s) of both the football and soccer teams were suspended from school grounds. As a result, they disclosed my sexual orientation to the entire student body. The captain of the soccer team was infuriated that school officials would not allow him to participate in the soccer conference championship.

Although both students were punished for their deplorable acts, my life wasn't easy. For several months I thought I was worth nothing. Students across my high school would laugh at me as if my existence was a joke. Athletes would shout that I was a *"fagot"* who did not have enough masculinity to be tough-minded. Things became so bleak that I needed an escort to walk me from class to class because I was afraid of being physically attacked. As a special education student, I felt violated and angry throughout high school because people blamed me for my sexual orientation. For roughly three years I decided to lock that skeleton in my closet and focus on other issues.

16

Discovering a Great Community

Since I was in middle school I felt removed from most students. The differences I encountered growing up (which included my learning disability and sexual orientation) isolated me from most of my colleagues. As early as the age of thirteen I initiated a goal that someday I would move far away. I even voiced my feelings to Cheryl by saying, "I am going to move *far away* someday." Even though I voiced my feelings to school staff—many people didn't take me seriously. Since I was only thirteen years old, many people thought I lacked the maturity to not only form personal goals, but live up to them as I aged into an adult.

Well before I started high school I developed a deep appreciation for the environment. During my childhood I went to great lengths to ensure my household recycled. My interest in recycling caused me to discover ways to making communities more sustainable. Since I was young, I wanted to join a profession that incorporated subjects I cared about (such as environmental science, community development, and public policy).

I discovered the planning profession during my sophomore year of high school. In 2006 I took a class called Career Awareness. My teacher Catherine Wright was highly influential because she helped me discover a profession that matched my interests. Before her class ended I researched education and job opportunities in urban planning. I really enjoyed the fact city planning not only allowed me to improve communities across Connecticut, but launch a career in public service.

When I was young I built a strong kinship with a town called West Hartford. Throughout my childhood I spent several summers in this community. During high school I made secret trips to a secluded reservoir located along the foothills of Avon Mountain. This park is truly a special place because it encompasses 3,000 acres of pristine forest. In addition, there are more than thirty miles of trails for walkers and bicyclists (which span across three quaint New England towns). The best time to visit this area is during the peak of Autumn because countless trees radiate warm colors against a crisp blue sky.

One Saturday afternoon I sat by myself for several minutes in front of this glistening reservoir. As I watched the sun beam its energy against this remarkable body of water, I removed myself from reality. I used this space to escape the constant hostility I was subject to on a daily basis. This reservoir served as my retreat center because it allowed me to leave behind my problems.

The positive energy I received whenever I traveled to West Hartford caused me to research the town's planning department. In March 2007 I contacted Mila Limson, the Senior Planner. Since I deeply cared about the vitality of this special community, I wanted to provide my service to help make West Hartford a better place. Several weeks before Spring Break I e-mailed Mila to schedule a meeting because I wanted to discuss career opportunities in urban planning.

Shortly after contacting Mila, I was convinced she would ignore my inquiry. Several days passed and I never heard from her.

One evening while sitting upstairs in my cozy study, I encountered a big surprise. The myth my imagination constructed over the past week was quickly shattered because Mila's name appeared inside my inbox.

Once I opened her e-mail, I *timidly* read through her response. As I finished reading this brief message, I gradually became optimistic that I could work with her someday. Mila ended by asking; "What time is best for us to meet and discuss career opportunities in the planning profession?"

As soon as I read her final sentence—I was thrilled. I ran downstairs and told my mother, *"The Senior Planner for the Town of West Hartford just reached out to me and wants to schedule a meeting during Spring Break!"*

I met with Mila in late April 2007. During this meeting I prepared numerous questions and did my best to take as many notes. My conversation with her was highly useful and lasted for over an hour. She was pleasantly surprised by my knowledge and enthusiasm of the planning profession. Before I left, I noticed several lawyers were waiting outside her office. Just before I stepped outside Mila's door, she told me to contact her once I enrolled in college because she would offer me an internship.

Once I secured an internship with Mila's office, I started researching schools that offered degrees in city planning. After searching through the *Planning Accreditation Board* website, I realized no colleges in Connecticut offered the major I was looking for. In order to pursue my academic dreams—I had to leave Connecticut.

Empire State: All Dressed Up and Nowhere to Go

Throughout life too many people are "all dressed up but have nowhere to go." On April 21, 2008 my older sister and I drove to New York City to visit Columbia University. I scheduled a campus tour with Columbia because it's not only home to one of the oldest planning programs in the country, but this campus is situated between Manhattan's Upper West Side and Harlem.

I was drawn to pursuing my undergraduate studies in New York because this city faced several interesting issues. In recent years, Harlem has undergone extensive revitalization. As a result, more and more affluent households are moving into this neighborhood. Another reason I found New York City appealing was that it's the world's 24th most populous city. Spending my college career in New York would help me acquire numerous career opportunities in urban planning.

Before my trip to the Big Apple I dressed for success. My parents bought me a colorful pair of Ralph Lauren shoes. These shoes were *boldly* checkered with each color of the rainbow. The night before my campus tour, I packed a lunch and selected the perfect outfit. I couldn't sleep. I fantasized about meeting a handsome Jewish guy, encountering Hillary Clinton at Starbucks, and arriving on the set of *Friends* (my favorite television show).

At 5:00 am my alarm went off to Janet Jackson's song entitled "So Excited." I chose her song to start my morning because my adrenaline levels were off the charts. I was beaming with joy because I finally had the opportunity to escape my hometown. Although I was ready to leave well before 7:00 am, my older sister Danielle spent over an hour perming her hair and applying makeup. There is no question she enjoys taking her time. After waiting for almost an eternity we finally drove off at 7:35 am.

My iPod was jamming to Daft Punk's single "One More Time." During this song's climax our vehicle raced across the state line. I felt a sudden burst of excitement as I *yelled* (in the most high pitch voice): *"Yes...we're in New York!"*

Once Danielle and I traveled into Manhattan we drove onto the Henry Hudson Parkway. I was greeted with jaw-dropping views of the Hudson River. My windshield transformed into a magical lens, which submerged our car beneath the George Washington Bridge.

As the sun beamed across the Hudson River, skylines of New York and New Jersey emerged directly in front of me. Each corner of the George Washington Bridge was wrapped with lush layers of green vegetation.

After struggling to find a parking spot, Danielle parked her car along W. 116th Street. Just before I opened my door I was celebrating because my patience finally paid off.

Once I stepped outside the first words I said were, *"This is really cool!"* My sister quickly muttered, *"Quiet!* Act like a normal person...the police department will come after you if you act up!"

I couldn't repress my emotions because I was living my childhood dream. Moving to another state was something I yearned for several years because it allowed me to start over. As I journeyed my surroundings, I developed a serious connection to this area. My favorite part about New York was the city's fast-pace and upbeat atmosphere.

Another reason I fell in love with New York was the fact Hillary Clinton would become my United States Senator. Throughout high school I looked up to progressive women because gay men were mostly nonexistent in politics. Even though gay men remain politically powerless, I was gratified to learn New York elected a staunch ally. I deeply admired Senator Clinton because she is a feminist. Residing in a state that is governed by feminists solidified my personal comfort because I knew those leaders are more sympathetic towards the needs and priorities of the gay community. Before I left New York I wanted to stop by Senator Clinton's office to thank her for advancing the rights of gays and lesbians at the national level.

Despite the fact I intended to stay in New York City, my adventure was unexpectedly cut short once my sister pulled me aside and told me we *had* to return to Connecticut. At first I did my best to resist her decision, however she used a three-line whip, which obliged me to walk back to her car. After spending $35 on gasoline I felt gypped to only experience New York City for two hours. There were so many things I wanted to accomplish before the end of the day.

Later that afternoon I realized my journey wasn't finished. I spent the next twelve months applying to colleges that offered degrees in city planning. When I was seventeen years old I determined New York City would someday be my new home. I was ready to spend the rest of my life in the Big Apple because Governor Patterson issued an Executive Order (in May 2008) directing state agencies to fully recognize same-sex marriages performed out-of-state. New York provided something Connecticut didn't offer and that was being treated like everyone else. Six months after visiting Columbia University my dream of residing in a state that extends marriage rights to same-sex couples came true.

3 POLITICAL JOURNEY BEGINS

"We can't expect to ride the wave if we aren't even willing to catch it."
-Jake Ducey

October 10, 2008 changed my life because it was the day I came across the headline "Gay Marriage Legal in Connecticut" in the *Hartford Courant*. Once I discovered this news I was elated because I never envisioned in my lifetime that I would ever enjoy the possibility of getting married. Nearly three years after my traumatic bullying incident the Connecticut Supreme Court issued a landmark ruling which paved the way for same-sex marriage. A sharply divided court determined 4-3 (in *Kerrigan v. Commissioner of Public Health*) that Connecticut's statutory ban on same-sex marriage was unconstitutional.

In the majority opinion, the justices not only challenged states which outlawed same-sex marriage, but they questioned the legitimacy of religious authority to discriminate against an entire subculture. Since most state constitutions prohibit same-sex marriage, the high court expressed deep concern over the well-being of gays and lesbians. In their ruling the court identified the parties responsible for stigmatizing the LGBT community in modern society and politics. The court specifically stated the overstepping between church and state occurred too many times:

> "The condemnation [of homosexuality] has been shaped by religious beliefs, conceptions of right and acceptable behavior, and respect for the traditional

> family. For many persons these are not trivial concerns
> but profound and deep convictions accepted as ethical
> and moral principles to which they aspire and which
> thus determine the course of their lives."

The Connecticut Supreme Court determined that religious authority *was* the origin of discrimination against the LGBT community. Furthermore, the justices expressed that religious groups *do not* have a right to impose their beliefs over the well-being of others. This ruling was tactful because it indicated that the few churches that support gay marriage had little clout in the political process and were often silenced by more conservative organizations. Additionally, the high court mentioned that special interests dictated the dialogue of this issue. The court's ruling was aggressive because it stated that homosexuals "remain a political underclass in our [state and] nation." Specifically the majority justices stated how throughout the world LGBT people are forced to live in fear:

> "Due to the harsh penalties imposed by society on
> persons identified as homosexual, many homosexual
> persons conceal their sexual orientation. Silence
> however, has its cost. It may allow a given individual to
> escape from the discrimination, abuse, and even
> violence which is often directed at homosexuals, but it
> ensures that homosexuals as a group are unheard
> politically."

The Connecticut Supreme Court did not hesitate to articulate the fact gays and lesbians are subject to widespread discrimination. The high court issued a firm decision upholding justice and human rights. This ruling is really powerful and meant a lot to me for many reasons. The court's decision determined that discrimination against gays and lesbians is wrong. In addition, Connecticut's highest court affirmed that religious values alone *do not* make it permissible to harm someone because of their sexual orientation. This ruling stuck down social constructs and empowered others to live freely. Being in a same-sex relationship was no longer a liability because Connecticut's legal system was transitioning towards full equality.

Defeating Question 1

The decision by Connecticut's highest court to legalize same-sex marriage came less than four weeks before Election Day. Although I was initially ecstatic, conservatives were motivated to use this ruling as an opportunity to not only turn out their political base, but many were eager to expunge same-sex marriage before it went into effect.

Connecticut voters are automatically asked every twenty years whether the state constitution should be revised or amended. Roughly three weeks after the state supreme court addressed one of the most polarizing political issues in the country, voters in Connecticut would weigh on whether to hold a Constitutional Convention.

Many Republicans used the *Kerrigan v. Commissioner of Public Health* ruling as a political football because they needed to pass Question 1 in order to have any chance at overturning same-sex marriage. Both Democrats and Republicans agreed that Question 1 was a crucial indicator on how Connecticut's future would be defined. If Question 1 was rejected it meant that gay marriage was going to stay. Defeating Question 1 was extremely important because it would set the stage for future same-sex marriage battles across America.

If voters approved Question 1, a Constitutional Convention would be held and delegates selected by the legislature would have the opportunity to put a same-sex marriage ban on the ballot. During this time voters in California were weighing on Proposition 8. Unlike the Proposition 8 campaign, which lasted for nearly six months, conservatives had less than four weeks to not only launch a statewide campaign, but sway an entire electorate to change the state constitution. A major advantage for proponents of same-sex marriage was that conservatives had no need to amend the Connecticut Constitution until the last minute.

The Connecticut Constitution has only been amended thirty times and has been in existence since 1965 when voters decided to replace their first constitution (which dated back to 1818). The last time voters amended the Connecticut Constitution was in 2000. The Connecticut Constitution is a *fragile* document and any modification deserves intense scrutiny.

I fought against Question 1 because there was no room to

embed discrimination in the Connecticut Constitution. In the weeks leading up to Election Day, I found myself sandwiched in a campaign of political warfare. The Catholic Church and Family Institute of Connecticut released misleading television ads persuading people to, "vote on major issues in our state." The Catholic Church failed to mention that the policies they were promoting discarded protections for women, students, homosexuals, and public employees across Connecticut.

Conservatives across the state including Cheryl worked to eradicate my rights. It was difficult enough losing a three-year friendship with someone I trusted, but it was unimaginable knowing someone was campaigning against me on a statewide referendum.

The bullying I experienced in high school reminded me of the bullying I witnessed gays and lesbians encounter during the campaign. Never in my life had I seen so many people use their faith as a political football to dehumanize others. I was enraged that people I knew (for several years) were convincing the public to vote against the interests of people they never met. Although my paraprofessional was campaigning against me, I was not going to sit back and watch her eat popcorn while the rights of thousands were being stripped away.

I quickly fought back because I was determined to do my part to defeat Question 1. I started my campaign against this issue by organizing employees within my high school. Although I was not old enough to vote, I campaigned against Question 1 because I wanted same-sex marriage to be legal in my home state. In late October I spoke to college students, older voters, and even convinced my high school guidance counselor to reject Question 1.

A week before the election, the state's largest newspaper featured an editorial *condemning* the measure. The League of Women Voters, Attorney General, and several constitutional scholars denounced Question 1. Despite the outpour in religious opposition to same-sex marriage, seventy clergy members across Connecticut petitioned against the Constitutional Convention.

I was really concerned heading into the 2008 election because I knew a lot of outside money was being spent on this race. On the eve of the election I was extremely stressed. I choked back tears inside my bedroom for several minutes because I was not sure if my rights would be left intact after the election. I told myself,

"Regardless of the outcome, I will not stop fighting for equal rights!" I was not ready to give in or give up fighting for others.

Moment of Truth

November 4, 2008 was the moment of truth. I was bracing for a very long election night because I knew it was full of several close races. During that evening I ran upstairs to watch election coverage on MSNBC. I stayed up late to watch President Obama deliver his victory speech in Chicago's Grant Park. Thousands of people flocked to Grant Park to celebrate the election of the country's first African American President. At around 11:45 pm I was exhausted. Although the results of Question 1 and Proposition 8 were not yet determined, I did not have the strength to remain awake all night. I went to bed hoping for the best because I needed to put on a strong face the following day.

On the morning after election night, I walked downstairs to cook some breakfast. My father approached me while I was sitting near the kitchen island and mentioned, "Question 1 was defeated by nearly 60%." When he first shared this news I thought he was joking.

Before I finished my breakfast, I ran upstairs and turned on my computer. I went online to research the election results. As I browsed through the Secretary of State's website, I realized my father was in fact correct. Of the 169 cities and towns in Connecticut, only five voted in favor of Question 1.

Despite the fact I was bullied on a regular basis, my outlook on life changed tremendously because voters and courts upheld my rights. Once I witnessed the final results, I was thrilled. I felt incredibly gratified to have friends who were willing to vote on my behalf. I was really happy to do my part to stop Question 1. At that moment, I realized someone believed in me, and that I had an opportunity to live my life like everyone else.

Election Aftermath

After surviving the biggest political earthquake of my life, I began picking up the pieces of broken friendships and looked back at what happened over the past three years. For the first time I seriously questioned authority. I started to doubt people who lacked any serious expertise. *Kerrigan v. Commissioner of Public Health* was decided by a group of legal experts who were tasked to not only defend the Constitution of Connecticut, but protect the welfare of others. This case was decided for a reason and there was an unknowable truth I struggled to wrap my arms around. Whenever I review a piece of legislation I examine it with close scrutiny. I not only review public policy with close scrutiny, but I want to understand the people behind any legislative proposal. When my paraprofessional supported an amendment to the Connecticut Constitution that eliminated same-sex marriage, I examined her ideas just as critically as I did her character.

For the next several days I reflected back on my experience with my paraprofessional to understand if she really was an informed citizen. Throughout this time I asked myself, "Does Cheryl recognize that *no country* in this world is immune from oppression, corruption, or discrimination? Why does she want to take away the rights of innocent people?"

My paraprofessional was never civic-minded until the Connecticut Assembly passed civil unions in 2005. Although she was a registered Republican for several years, she could not identify her own Governor on a photo lineup. On one occasion I showed her a picture of Governor Rell when she was featured in the newspaper. When I first pointed to Governor Rell's image she said, *"Wow...this is the first time I have ever seen her. I didn't know Connecticut had a female Governor."* Even though I was not old enough to vote (at the age of fourteen), I acquired more knowledge of state government than someone who lived in Connecticut since 1968.

My Day of Enlightenment

As I drove home from school on the day before Thanksgiving, Cheryl's Lexus was stopped at a red light. This was the first time I saw her following the legalization of same-sex marriage in Connecticut. There was no question in my mind she was livid over the defeat of Question 1.

For just a few moments, I reflected on November 3, 2005. I thought to myself, "How could I transform my biggest loss in life into a virtue?" Throughout high school I was learning more and more about myself, however I wanted to find a career, which positioned me to become a catalyst for positive change. Before my eighteenth birthday, I was determined to do my part to make the world a better place. In addition, I wanted to devote my career towards reversing injustices that I encountered. During the next several hours I secluded myself from friends and family members because I underwent a period of political enlightenment.

A giant light bulb went off inside my head on the morning of November 27, 2008. Once I stepped outside the shower I experienced an epiphany. As I listened to Duncan Sheik's song "Barley Breathing," I finally came to the realization that my paraprofessional and many other students (who bullied me) were wrong.

For over three years I surrounded myself with individuals who did not care about my existence. When I was fourteen years old my brain did not fully mature. As a result, I was more vulnerable to being influenced by malign systems of thought. Throughout my childhood I lacked the confidence to question authority. I rarely defended my values because I was not informed. During high school, I never spent much time researching human rights. Until 2008, I was never aware Connecticut became the sixteenth jurisdiction in the world to legalize gay marriage. In addition, I never learned that a nation once governed under Apartheid was surpassing the United States when it came to equal rights.

Education is a powerful tool people use to change the world. Studying human rights legislation and same-sex marriage court decisions around the world became a pivotal ingredient that helped me undergo a radical transformation.

By November 27, 2008 five countries questioned authority. Same-sex marriage was permitted in the Netherlands, Belgium, Spain, Canada, and South Africa. If this policy is incredibly reprehensible why do conservatives vacation in places (such as Aruba) that contradict their beliefs? If extending basic rights to same-sex couples (such as hospital visitations or burial rights) is immoral why have more people not condemned progressive governments. "Why did my paraprofessional channel her political attacks on a fourteen-year-old high school student instead of protesting in front of Parliaments across the world?" If religious conservatives truly want to eliminate the rights of gays and lesbians they should have fought abroad many years ago. As soon as five countries made it permissible for gays and lesbians to get married, the truth was already unleashed.

During my freshman year of high school Melissa Perez (a longtime mentor) taught me the importance of separation between church and state. She explained how the world encompasses many types of faith. As a result, countries should not sponsor state religions because public policy must not favor certain faiths or customs. An important role of government is to embrace freedom of thought. Establishing a state religion is contrary to Article 18 listed in the United Nations International Covenant on Civil and Political Rights which, "mandates freedom of religion."

If the Constitution of Cambodia recognizes Buddhism as the only official religion and the Constitution of Egypt confirms, "The principles of Islamic Sharia are the main source of legislation." Why should one religion in this world supersede another? Throughout this time I asked myself, "Why are Protestants more credible than other faiths when it comes to influencing public policy?" If state religions are detrimental towards democracy, why do only a few faiths dominate political conversations? Although I have no expertise in religious studies, I questioned the authority of certain faiths. I wanted to understand *why* conservatives thrived whenever they imposed their beliefs over the well-being of others.

I came to a realization that God does not hate homosexuals. After learning sixteen jurisdictions across the world paved the way for same-sex couples to legally marry—I determined this issue was not about religion.

Sixteen jurisdictions recognized that gays and lesbians are subject to widespread discrimination. The actions of several court rulings and legislative reforms insist that past intolerance is no longer acceptable. I was not the only person who understood the social cost of oppression was far more destructive than upholding the beliefs of some faiths.

Albie Sachs started his career as a human rights activist when he was seventeen years old. Once he completed law school he fought vociferously to abolish capital punishment in South Africa. The bulk of his work involved defending people charged under racist statutes and repressive security laws. Throughout his career he campaigned against Apartheid. After being arrested and placed in solitary confinement for over five months, he moved to England where he lived in exile. While staying in Mozambique in 1988 he almost died when a car bomb was secretly installed by South African security agents.

In 1990 he returned to South Africa and served as a member of the Constitutional Committee. He played an instrumental role when it came to forging negotiations to end Apartheid. Shortly after Nelson Mandela was elected President of South Africa; he became appointed to serve on the Constitutional Court of South Africa. During his tenure, Justice Sachs presided over cases regarding the end of capital punishment and legalization of same-sex marriage. In a widely quoted passage from the *Minister of Home Affairs v. Fourie* ruling, Justice Sachs determined:

> "The exclusion of same-sex couples from the benefits and responsibilities of marriage, accordingly, is not a small and tangential inconvenience. It represents a harsh if oblique statement by the law that same-sex couples are outsiders, and that their need for affirmation and protection of their intimate relations as human beings is somehow less than that of heterosexual couples. It reinforces the wounding notion that they are to be treated as biological oddities, as failed or lapsed human beings who do not fit into normal society, and, as such, do not qualify for the full moral concern. It signifies that their capacity for love, commitment and accepting responsibility is by definition less worthy of regard than that of heterosexual couples."

Justice Sachs reiterated that I was not just another "lapsed human." The words from this ruling meant a lot to me because it affirmed that I do not have a lower capacity to love, commitment, and accept responsibility for another person. At that moment I realized gays and lesbians are not "biological oddities." I choked back tears for the next several minutes while I sat in my bedroom. My face was covered in tears because it marked the first time I felt content in my own skin. I repeatedly exclaimed, *"I am who I am, and people need to accept it!"* I ran into the nearest bathroom and grabbed large swaths of toilet paper. The pain I repressed for over three years was finally beginning to heal because I was transforming into a champion for human rights.

The thoughts and ideas I envisioned during this period became the foundation for my political message across the country. I come across my best ideas through a combination of intuition and feeling. I had to *feel* the pain of watching countless people feel rejected by their own government before I was inspired to enter politics. Before I was ready to fight on the front lines, I removed myself from others in order to fully comprehend my complex ideas.

The morning of November 27, 2008 was crucial because it allowed me to conjure radical ideas and outline how I was going to articulate a strong message. The reason it took me longer to formulate my concepts was that I was not only trying understand the existing political landscape for gays and lesbians, but I had to create a plan which allowed my ideas to tactfully fit into public policy. I was required to steadily work within the system if I wanted to advance meaningful reforms.

Since undergoing this epiphany, I became *obsessed* with political analysis. Throughout high school I would retreat upstairs into a cozy study and shut others out. I did not want anybody to know what I was doing because my ideas were too complex for most individuals to understand. I spoke in such detail that many people believed I missed the big picture. I initially experienced great difficulty understanding how I reached my own conclusions. Sometimes I spent several hours alone talking to myself aloud because I needed to learn how to fully justify and defend my concepts.

The first person I decided to share this moment with was Rachel Margolis. She was one of the first people I "came out" to regarding my sexual orientation. Rachel was incredibly supportive during my freshman year of high school. I felt more than comfortable sharing my deepest thoughts with her. Shortly after sneaking into an empty room upstairs, I compiled a brief, but detailed e-mail explaining that; "I *fully* intend to recycle my anger and frustration into motivation for equal rights. I'm *determined* to spread the same hope I was fortunate to receive across the nation."

Less than an hour after sending this message, I heard a rapid response. In all capitalize letters Rachel wrote: "GABRIEL, I'M SO PROUD OF YOU! LET'S TALK SOON. KEEP REACHING FOR THE STARS!!!"

November 27, 2008 changed my life because it marked the beginning of my political career. From that day forward, I used each day I lived as an opportunity to make the world a better place. I took action because I did not want to witness anymore innocent people be oppressed by their own government. Too many people were being deprived their citizenship on a daily basis. I was not going to sit back and watch this dire injustice persist.

I was inspired by same-sex marriage victories in Connecticut and Massachusetts. Once I returned to school, I woke up each morning as if it were November 27, 2008. I was determined to continue advancing the interests of this important social movement. I had no idea what would conspire over the next several months. On December 1, 2008 I heard a call to go forth into the world and help others. I was determined to rise to this occasion, even if it required me to sacrifice my own comfort.

4 BREAKING AN IMPASSE IN NORTH CAROLINA

"It is hard to fail, but it is worse never to have tried to succeed."
-Theodore Roosevelt

After the election I started to ventilate my frustration by taking my fight directly to the Republican establishment. I was not only disgusted at the party's platform, but there were people in positions of power who were working to suppress the voices of gays and lesbians. Since I was in high school I was aware that *many* bullies existed in the Republican Party. Furthermore, there were politicians who did not want me to make it and did not care if I lived in fear.

In December 2008 I contacted United States Senator Saxby Chambliss. Senator Chambliss is a staunch opponent of gay rights. He sponsored the Federal Marriage Amendment, which precluded states such as Connecticut and Massachusetts from recognizing same-sex marriage. In addition, Senator Chambliss voted against repealing Don't Ask, Don't Tell, which permitted gays, lesbians, and bisexuals to serve in the United States Military.

Senator Chambliss recently survived a tough re-election against Jim Martin. His race was so narrow it was forced into a runoff. Sarah Palin even had to fly to Georgia because many conservatives sensed his vulnerability. Shortly after winning the runoff election I started to protest against Senator Chambliss because I smelled blood. During my study hall I went into my guidance counselor's office because I wanted to protest the Republican establishment.

Melissa Warrek played the role of a second guidance counselor during my senior year of high school. Even though she was not the primary person I worked with in guidance, she was heavily instrumental when it came to helping me recycle past pain into political passion. Melissa was extremely kind because she allowed me to use her office as a phone banking center so I could hold my government accountable.

One afternoon I called the office of Senator Chambliss. At the age of seventeen I told his legislative assistant over the phone; "Senator Chambliss has done nothing but spread *ignorance* and *negativity* across Congress." Just after I made those remarks his assistant quickly became defensive. She initially denied claims that Senator Chambliss would ever spread ignorance, however I fired back by expressing that Senator Chambliss supports the Federal Marriage Amendment and was working to take my rights away.

Once she detected my sexual orientation she was prepared to end the conversation. During my final remarks I told her to tell Senator Chambliss that; *"He does not know me and has no business trying to turn my state against me! He needs to be thrown out of office and must stop obstructing gay rights!"*

For the first time, I found myself playing political defense. My home state had just legalized same-sex marriage and I was determined to make sure Connecticut never looked back. Shortly after the election I assumed an unofficial leadership role in the gay rights movement because I was one of a few individuals who was fortunate to live in a state that ensured full equality for gays and lesbians. I was determined to use this opportunity to not only defend the values of my home state, but I was going to expand my fight beyond the borders of Connecticut.

North Carolina's Political Landscape

Although *screaming* at conservatives over phone helped alleviate my frustration, I needed to play political offense in order to secure more victories for gay rights. Attacking the Republican Party and only playing defense would not help advance my overall goal of propelling same-sex marriage to the United States Supreme Court.

I decided to campaign for gay rights in a southern state because I was ready to capitalize on the Democratic tsunami. After several weeks of researching political geography, I discovered a list of southern states President Obama won. I examined states where Democrats enjoyed large majorities not only in state legislatures, but where they controlled the Governor's Mansion as well. I realized that Democrats were going to be a key partner in my fight for equality.

The three states I initially deliberated to start my legislative career were Florida, Virginia, and North Carolina. I first ruled out campaigning for same-sex marriage in Florida because voters recently approved Amendment 2 by a wide margin. Moreover, I was disgusted at the fact the Governor not only opposed same-sex marriage, but defended a lawsuit which prohibited same-sex couples from jointly adopting. Trying to convince a Governor to not only stop defending a Florida law in state court, but support changing the Florida Constitution was an incredible obstacle. Additionally, I was ominous that a Republican dominated legislature would even support a gay rights bill.

When it came to Virginia I was also skeptical. Just two years ago voters approved the Marshall-Newman Amendment. This policy forbids *any* recognition of private contracts between same-sex couples (even if they were legally married in another jurisdiction). Despite the fact that Democrats controlled the Virginia Senate and Governor's Mansion, Republicans ruled the House of Delegates with an iron fist. My fight would not only involve repealing Virginia's same-sex marriage ban, but it also required the General Assembly to pass a gender-neutral marriage statue. Repealing a constitutional amendment and passing a separate piece of controversial legislation would be a very tall order for any seventeen-year-old high school student. In less than a year I was going off to college. I believed that securing enough votes and convincing a Governor to amend a state constitution would take too much time. Once I studied Virginia's political landscape, I realized that legislative gridlock would not favor the innovative ideas I wanted to champion.

My last hope was North Carolina. Although North Carolina was by far the most conservative state I researched, Republicans faced a twenty-year gubernatorial losing streak. Only two Republicans were elected Governor since 1902. What was even more encouraging was that Democrats controlled the legislature since 1896. 2008 was a historic election in North Carolina because voters elected their first female Governor Beverly Perdue.

Governor Perdue was a champion for education. She supported legislation that would admit every high school student in North Carolina into a community college tuition-free. When she served as Lieutenant Governor, she cast the tie-breaking vote, which established the North Carolina Education Lottery.

What made North Carolina so appealing was that it was the only southern state to never enact a constitutional ban on same-sex marriage. If I wanted to spread the same hope I was fortunate to receive—I only needed to secure a simple majority vote in the legislature. Once I solidified enough support, a marriage bill would be sent to the Governor's desk and history would happen just like it did in Connecticut.

Despite the fact North Carolina is located in the heart of the Bible Belt, I believed that my experience in high school could compel anyone (regardless of political beliefs) to support same-sex marriage. On December 17, 2008 I started contacting lawmakers in North Carolina. On several occasions I secretly entered my guidance counselor's office (when she was assigned to lunch duty) to fight for same-sex marriage. At times I would turn off the lights because I did not want *anyone* to notice my activities. Once I entered the room I picked up her phone and called an extensive list of state lawmakers and organizations across North Carolina. Study hall was the only opportunity I had to advance gay rights because I was also applying to colleges and participating on my high school swim team.

Throughout high school I kept my eye on the prize. I was the type of student who would forgo a pleasure of the moment in order to prepare for legislative history. I knew safe in the knowledge one day someone might thank me for my dedication to helping others. Most people my age spent Friday night going to the movie theater or attending house parties, but I was determined to build a robust list of organizations and lawmakers I needed to advance gay rights in North Carolina. I invested numerous Friday nights developing strategies on how to successfully reach out to various political organizations and state lawmakers. This small idea eventually transformed into a major social movement which stretched into seven states, broke a forty-year legislative impasse, and caused ten states to modify the way they address violence in public schools.

Calling state lawmakers in North Carolina was my only opportunity to ensure my voice was heard. In the first week, I received mixed receptions about the idea of legalizing same-sex marriage. Regardless of the legislative outcome, I was *determined* to start an important conversation. There were times I was laughed at by legislative staff for proposing same sex marriage. Despite the challenges I faced trying to efface a stigma, my conversations in North Carolina carried a greater meaning. I was not only trying to change a state law, but I did my best to normalize a controversial issue most people never knew existed.

Nelson Mandela released a famous quote that emphasizes the importance of knowledge; "Education is the most powerful weapon which you can use to change the world." Towards the end of 2008, I was applying the knowledge I acquired in the aftermath of *Kerrigan v. Commissioner of Public Health* to demonstrate that homosexuals are not going to remain an invisible minority. I felt comfortable justifying *why* living in a place where I enjoy basic rights made me a better person. In addition, I was not going to allow past mistakes or political barriers define the future of the gay rights movement.

Throughout the 1990s many states and the federal government were rescinding the rights of gays and lesbians. It started when President Bill Clinton signed laws such as the Defense of Marriage Act and Don't Ask Don't Tell. The HIV/AIDS epidemic did little to quell the stigma many men in same-sex relationships face. As a result, many gay men were pressured to conceal their identity. The social activities embedded in gay culture (such as gay bars and bathhouses) were often hidden from society. Silence became a major reason gay men had almost no clout in the political process.

During my early teenage years gay men were practically nonexistent in many state governments. When I started my journey in politics I asked myself, "Where are the gay men?" Since gay men were not serving in the North Carolina legislature I had to do my best to represent the values and goals of this community. I felt even more pressure to represent the gay community at-large because I was fortunate to live in one of two states that permitted same-sex marriage. I had an opportunity that most gay men did not have which was that my state's legal system ensured full equality. Furthermore, I wanted to send a message to the people of North

Carolina that my sexual orientation does not hinder my ability to be a productive member of society.

Meeting Chardon Murray

On the day before Christmas vacation I called a long list of lawmakers. I had to pack as many phone calls because I would not return to Melissa's office until the following month. During that afternoon many offices didn't answer. Although I was initially discouraged that I would not speak to a real person, I decided to persist because I knew my hard work would pay off. As I went down my contact list, I came across State Senator Julia Boseman.

Shortly before the day ended, I called her office. A young woman picked up the phone and spoke with a southern accent. Her name was Chardon Murray and she worked as the Legislative Aide for Senator Boseman. Chardon is a lifelong resident of North Carolina and seemed surprised that her office received a call from a Connecticut high school student. I initially laughed when I heard her voice because I was no longer in Connecticut. Calling her office was truly a moment of consequence because I had no clue that Senator Boseman was the first LGBT lawmaker in North Carolina. During the beginning this intense conversation I expressed in a *shallow* voice why I was reaching out to Senator Boseman:

> "My name is Gabriel and I'm a seventeen-year-old high school student from Connecticut. Last month my home state legalized same-sex marriage. When I was three years old I was diagnosed with autism. As a result, I've relied on a paraprofessional to help me with daily activities. Since I was eleven years old I developed a very close friendship with this individual. During the eighth grade she brainwashed me by calling homosexuals *"disgusting."* In addition, she notified me that she would put her *own* children up for adoption if any were gay.
>
> *I'm calling your office because I don't have any friends. I have nothing to lose.* Connecticut *just* legalized same-sex marriage and I want to spread the same hope I was fortunate to receive. I'm turning my greatest loss in life into a virtue because I'm *determined* to fight for equality. I want the North Carolina legislature to pass same-sex

marriage so they can send a message to other states that discrimination is *wrong*."

Chardon was astonished by how well I recalled my freshman year. My story caused her to cry over the phone. Once I finished speaking, she responded in such a heavy voice:

"Let me say this, *"I'm amazed at how far you've come!"* You are going to do great things in your life. Even though Connecticut legalized same-sex marriage, Democrats in North Carolina aren't progressive compared to the Northeast. Our state has never discussed this issue because we simply *aren't there yet*. Last year an anti-bullying bill died in the legislature because Republicans threatened to oust any Democrat who supported it.

There was a *real* chance same-sex marriage could win in California. Of the three states that voted to ban same-sex marriage, there was a possibility Proposition 8 would fail. Proposition 8 passed even when Democrats enjoy a great election cycle. The point I want to make is that even in liberal states, same-sex marriage has not prevailed."

Instead of celebrating the victory of same-sex marriage in Connecticut, much of the national attention was focused on the tragic outcomes of statewide ballot measures. Although gay rights activists across the country were shaken by the passage of Proposition 8—I was determined to move forward. Towards the end of this profound discussion Chardon indicated that even though same-sex marriage will not be included on this year's legislative agenda—Senator Boseman plans to re-introduce the School Violence Prevention Act next month.

School Violence Prevention Act

Senator Boseman was elected to the State Senate in 2004 and represents a small district outside Wilmington. Since 2005 she has introduced the School Violence Prevention Act (SB 526). This provision would require school districts in North Carolina to adopt a comprehensive anti-bullying policy using enumerated categories such as gender identity, race, religion, age, and sexual orientation.

Although my initial goal was to advocate for same-sex marriage, I decided that pursuing SB 526 would be more feasible because this bill was introduced on several occasions. In addition, I would be able to facilitate a conversation that already existed in state government.

During my first conversation, Chardon promised to send me important information pertaining to gay rights. Several days passed and I never heard from her. I quickly became suspicious and decided to contact Senator Boseman's office in early January. Once I e-mailed Senator Boseman's office, Chardon responded to my inquiry and notified me that she had lost my contact information.

Chardon was *very* thankful I reached out because she wasn't sure if she would hear from me again. Writing to Senator Boseman was truly a blessing in disguise. Had I not reached out to her, my story would have never made it to the North Carolina legislature.

After going back and forth between Chardon, I contacted Ian Palmquist, the Executive Director of Equality North Carolina. The primary focus of Equality North Carolina is to advance LGBT legislation within state and local government. I asked him what I could do to help advance SB 526 and help other students who are struggling to come to terms with their sexual identity. After speaking with Palmquist I realized that talking to people individually was not enough.

Chardon informed me earlier that her friend, Bambi Weavil, was the editor of *Out Impact Magazine*. This publication is a gay online magazine based in New York City. Her close friend from college launched *Out Impact Magazine* in June 2007 to post information regarding events, entertainment, and political stories within the gay community. Chardon suggested that she would be willing to pass along my story to *Out Impact* so it could gain a larger audience. Using this website would provide the megaphone needed to transmit my ideas to a large audience.

Although I was never elected to public office, I was a great writer. During my bullying incident in 2005 I had to write a detailed report describing the entire incident to the Vice Principal. My arguments were framed in such a powerful manner that I managed to suspend the captain(s) of the high school football and soccer team(s). In the past writing has provided me the platform to take on powerful interests. I was confident that I could channel the same energy I felt in my bullying report once I drafted this blog.

On January 23, 2009 I decided to break my silence. After locking countless skeletons inside my closet for three years I was determined to not let past mistakes define my identity and character. During that Friday afternoon I went into the classroom of Nicole Charles (who taught History) and spent a couple of hours writing my story. My objective was to detail as much information and discuss what happened to me on November 3, 2005. I had to reveal the *worst* day of my life to an entire state legislature.

While writing this story, my thoughts and emotions poured fluidly onto paper. The process of articulating my bullying experience felt like basic instinct. I was able to compose a long, detailed, and rich analysis of several situations, which involved being taken advantage of by my peers. As I was typing this story I expressed the moment I saw the captain of the football team laugh as if my existence was a joke. I explained how one student stole my lunch on a regular basis and demanded that I disclosed something about my sexual orientation.

Although I was pouring my heart into this graphic testimony there was one thing I left out. In my testimony I mentioned, "I had little hope that I would make it." Throughout high school I experienced many cycles of severe depression. The first stages of my depression involved me throwing away many personal belongings. In the weeks leading up to my bullying incident I gradually stopped taking care of myself because I did not intend residing anywhere long-term. On the evening of November 3, 2005 I attempted suicide. I went into my medicine cabinet and mixed a toxic combination of controlled substances, painkillers, and antidepressants. I attempted to kill myself because I was ready to detach myself from my own body. Seeing darkness did not scare me because I no longer liked who I was.

Although I was on my way out, there was someone with me that evening. Her name was Melissa Perez and she became instrumental when it came to helping me during that perilous moment. Melissa convinced me to not hurt myself (any further). She assured me that she would help me overcome any personal grief or depression. What made me listen to her was when she told me about the time she was threatened during the seventh grade. She told me about the moment someone in her middle school threatened her life and how she acquired the strength to overcome those personal challenges. She explained how her worst day transformed her into a better individual. Melissa Perez talked me out of hurting myself and I would not be around without her support that evening. She told me that November 3, 2005 was not my final day on earth and she was correct.

For just a moment, I understood that the pain I experienced gave me the strength of will and strength of emotion to fight for others. The hardships I encountered three years ago prepared me to advance SB 526. I did not explicitly mention my suicide attempt in my written testimony because I did not feel comfortable using such graphic language. I also did not want my suicide attempt to diminish my credibility or compromise the chances of this bill's success.

I was using Nicole Charles's classroom to help students who felt that they did not have a purpose in life. This was my opportunity to heal a major conflict that divided social groups in North Carolina. I was fortunate that I was still alive to share this story because many people in my situation might not have made it.

As I finished writing, I positioned my final arguments by appealing to as many people as possible. After proofreading my story, I had no idea what would conspire once I pressed the "send" button on my e-mail browser. The story I shared to *Out Impact Magazine* eventually became a crucial ingredient to winning the hearts and minds of many state lawmakers.

Later that night, I received an e-mail from Bambi Weavil. She expressed her appreciation and gratitude for having me share my story. I remember feeling flattered because it was the first time someone read it. I choked back tears thinking that I had a real chance at making a positive difference. Bambi informed me that her and Chardon were deeply impressed. She ensured; "many important eyes will see what you wrote." Shortly after my blog went viral, the conversation of SB 526 shifted in a different direction.

As my story gained popularity across North Carolina, the chances that SB 526 would someday be sent to Governor Perdue's desk dramatically increased. By March 2009 my message circulated around North Carolina. Polling conducted by *Public Policy Polling* indicated that 69% of North Carolina voters supported the School Violence Prevention Act with the sexual orientation clause included. According to *Public Policy Polling*, 51% of Republicans in

North Carolina supported this measure. This was the first time in recent memory that I had witnessed Republicans support a gay rights measure. I contacted Rachel Margolis, a close friend I knew from North Carolina. I told her how support for SB 526 has grown significantly within the past few months. I notified her there was a real chance this legislation could pass.

Shortly after my blog circulated a broad coalition of students, teachers, parents, and community activists organized the *Prevent School Violence in North Carolina* campaign to demonstrate support for SB 526. A few months after my blog was published, several students across North Carolina began sharing their stories. I saw an outpour of students and young people demand their state government take action. For several years the Republican Party has blocked SB 526 because it "legitimizes homosexuality" however the public outcry in North Carolina sent an urgent message to the legislature that change is needed.

The North Carolina State Senate began debating the School Violence Prevention Act in March 2009 and passed it in May. Once SB 526 survived the Upper House, all eyes were focused on the House of Representatives. Many Democrats in Raleigh were not certain if the School Violence Prevention Act would clear the lower chamber. While lawmakers were debating the School Violence Prevention Act, I was preparing for my high school graduation. The end of June was very nerve-wracking. The School Violence Prevention Act was a *very* controversial bill. This issue sparked emotions from both Democrats and Republicans. Hearings and testimony for this bill lasted for several hours. I remember feeling anxious because I realized my political ambitions were being put to a major test.

The debates regarding SB 526 were really harsh. Many conservatives used the hearings in the House of Representatives as an opportunity to state vile remarks against homosexuals. One Republican lawmaker claimed that, "same-sex marriage is worse than secondhand smoke." The crude statements being said on the legislative floor largely ignored the true victims in North Carolina schools. What bothered me most about the Republican Caucus was the fact they were more concerned about gay sex than protecting students from violence. The legislative floor became a chat room for sexually charged issues.

The School Violence Prevention Act narrowly passed the North

Carolina General Assembly despite initial push back. On June 23, 2009 just two days before my high school graduation the House of Representatives voted 58-57. Speaker of the House Joe Hackney was the tiebreaker and deciding vote. Two Republicans missed the vote and Democrats tactfully scheduled the final vote once they both left Raleigh.

I was both surprised and elated to discover that SB 526 had passed. I choked back tears once I knew that I managed to turn a difficult experience into a virtue. On June 30, 2009 North Carolina Governor Beverly Perdue signed SB 526 into law making North Carolina the ninth state to enact comprehensive anti-bullying legislation. Before I graduated high school, I was able to pass a gay rights bill in North Carolina and break a forty-year legislative impasse. This experience was truly rewarding because it demonstrated my commitment to helping students across North Carolina. It also inspired me to continue my fight for equality and human dignity.

5 DETERMINED TO LEAVE

"I take responsibility for my life, and if I have the will to do something, that can override talent, the past, whatever it is."
-Jake Ducey

On April 2, 2009 I was crushed to receive my rejection letter from New York University. For roughly an hour I couldn't put down that letter because I invested so much effort trying to secure a spot in that school. Despite the fact my high school class rank was 6 (out of over 300 students), I was not able to carry the ball over the finish line. If testifying in favor of a gay rights bill and overcoming a learning disability could not secure a spot into New York University, I had no clue what would launch me into the Big Apple. Shortly after reading my rejection letter I realized it wasn't the right time to move away.

Before my high school graduation I decided to enroll at the University of Connecticut (UConn). Shortly after sending my admission deposit to UConn, a friend of mine from Wesleyan University was studying at the University of Washington as a visiting non-matriculated student. One afternoon he e-mailed me the syllabus for UDP 300: Introduction to Urban Planning.

When I printed the syllabus I was amazed to see cutting edge concepts be incorporated into class curriculum. The term "utopian cities" immediately caught my attention. Studying "utopian cities" not only fascinated me, but it caused me to extensively research what the University of Washington had to offer.

My heart was first set on University of Washington as soon as I learned they offered both an undergraduate and graduate degree in urban planning. What I found even more impressive was the fact it's home to the third oldest planning program in the nation. In addition, it shared New York University's academic colors and UConn's athletic mascot. I really wanted to study in Seattle because I thought it would be an extraordinary opportunity to acquire professional experience. Furthermore, I believed it would increase my chances of being admitted into a prestigious graduate program.

The first time I learned about Seattle was in 2007 when I purchased a book written by Mark Hinshaw called, *True Urbanism: Living in and Near the Center*. The author not only lives in Seattle, but he sheds light on how the city encourages vibrant urban centers. The images featured in his book (of Seattle's modern skyline) encouraged me to warm up to the Emerald City.

One month before my high school graduation I told my guidance counselor, "Someday I'll be a Washington Husky!" He *laughed* at me in a belittling manner because he thought I was trying to fill a temporary void after being denied by New York University.

National Student Exchange

Before I mailed my admission deposit, I formulated a game plan to leave Connecticut. I spent my final weeks of high school exploring opportunities to pay in-state tuition while attending an out-of-state college.

Just before my high school graduation I came across the National Student Exchange. This program allowed me to study a full-year at the University of Washington and not pay *any* out-of-state tuition. In addition, I could use this experience to determine if I wanted to transfer. This opportunity was extremely lucrative because it was my ticket to starting over. My objective was to study at the University of Washington (as a visiting student) during my sophomore year and transfer junior year.

My freshman year of college was merely a stepping-stone (as soon as I arrived on campus I wanted to escape). Despite feeling stuck, I was determined to leave. During my first semester I met with the National Student Exchange coordinator Lisa McAdam Donegan to discuss how I could attend the University of Washington. Lisa was a close friend of Clay Schwenn, the

Exchange Coordinator for University of Washington. Before I left our meeting she assured; *"Don't worry*...I think I can secure you a spot at University of Washington. I'll *bribe Clay* with drinks at the national conference if need be!"

Even though my application prospects were rising, I experienced a major setback. Just before Winter Break I asked my advisor for a letter of recommendation. His first excuse was; "I *don't* typically write letters of recommendation for freshman because they are *least* experienced. If you were a junior that's a different story..."

Once I informed him I was applying to the National Student Exchange he *immediately* dismissed my desire to attend University of Washington.

The first negative tactic he used included my standardized test scores. My advisor critically asked, "What was *your* score on the SAT and ACT, did *you* even take the *exam?"* Once he learned I received a 23 on the ACT and 990 on SAT he expressed; "You'll *never* get accepted into University of Washington. *It's really competitive. Your* test scores *aren't* good. Besides, living in Seattle is *very expensive."*

Several weeks later, I convinced Christine Wenzel, the Associate Director of the Center for Students with Disabilities to send a letter of recommendation. During this time Christine played a major role when it came to helping me attend the University of Washington. Christine was incredibly supportive of my decision to move to Seattle. Furthermore, she was one of only a few people I trusted. Christine has a remarkable gift when it comes to putting people at ease and encouraging others to set high goals.

Hard Choices

During my freshman year of college my parents pressured me to become a Residential Advisor because they weren't certain if they could pay my tuition. After undergoing a rigorous interview in early March I was selected. Not only were my room expenses covered, but I was also offered a $4,000 stipend. This deal was extremely lucrative because it totaled at least $8,000. In addition, I could retain my job at a restaurant I really enjoyed.

Throughout spring semester I deliberated whether or not I was going to participate in the National Student Exchange or accept

$8,000. Although moving to Seattle would upset my parents, my heart and mind were already set.

Before my acceptance into the student exchange I decided to contact two individuals who could help reaffirm my decision to live in Washington. I first wrote to Emily Janes who is a native Washingtonian. Emily grew up in a small town outside Seattle. In addition, several of her friends graduated from University of Washington. During the application process she told me to, *"go with your gut."*

Another person I contacted was Sarah Showalter. A few years ago Sarah faced a similar dilemma. She was offered a full-ride to the University of Michigan, however she declined that opportunity to pursue a Master of City Planning at the University of Pennsylvania. Although Sarah incurred a significant amount of student loan debt, she reassured me that attending a school with a stronger department was, *"worth the extra cash."*

--

On March 19, 2010 I discovered *fantastic* news—I was accepted into the National Student Exchange. Once I realized I would be attending the University of Washington in September—*I was thrilled!*

This letter was not just about attending another school; it was about starting a new life. For the past six years I was forced to reside in a place where I was bullied and harassed on a regular basis—my acceptance into the National Student Exchange changed everything.

During the past six years I felt trapped. Six years seems so significant to many people my age because that's nearly one-third of our entire life. Think about how it feels to spend *one-third* of your life in a place that made you miserable? Imagine being forced to spend *one-third* of your life in a place you didn't want to be in.

In roughly six months I would start a new chapter. This venture was something I've *craved* since middle school. Leaving Connecticut has been my dream since I was thirteen years old and at the age of nineteen it was finally coming true.

6 STARTING OVER IN SEATTLE

"Do not go where the path may lead, go instead where there is no path and leave a trail."
-Ralph Waldo Emerson

September 21, 2010 was the day my dream became a reality—I packed up my bags and moved across country. The first obstacle I faced was enduring a *very* cold shower (at 2:30 am). Despite this chilly start, I was *ecstatic* to begin a new chapter. Before I left my house I hugged my mom and both my dogs. Shortly after, my father and I packed several suitcases before leaving in the middle of the night.

Once we arrived at Bradley Airport, the thought of leaving a place where I spent the past *nineteen years* began to set in. I was leaving a place I didn't think I would *ever* escape. As I waited for the airline worker to scan my boarding pass, a vibrant celebration occurred inside me. Since I was thirteen years old I dreamed of leaving my hometown. Despite the fact I wasn't accepted into New York University, I thought about the time I told my high school guidance counselor, *"Someday I'll be a Washington Husky!"* Even though I was bullied on a regular basis, I recalled the moment I informed my paraprofessional, "I am going to move *far away* someday."

I walked through the jet bridge content. I was ready to embark on new challenges and meet new friends. Even though past critics weren't there to witness what occurred—I fulfilled a *very* important promise. A few minutes before departure, tears raced down my face. I never envisioned that I would experience such a monumental day in my life. As soon as the plane approached the runway—I *finally* made it.

New Home

Eastern Washington is *very rural*—infinite stretches of flat terrain and high deserts extend for hundreds of miles. By 10:20 am our flight was preparing its final descent. My iPod was jamming to "Evacuate the Dance Floor" by Cascada. This single combines German pop vocals and techno beats to create a fast-pace soundtrack. Although the beginning is full of redundant rhythms— it foreshadows dramatic shifts. Towards the song's climax a sudden verse of rap lyrics unexpectedly twists the entire melody. This sudden change strikes a familiar shift in what I witnessed during my flight.

As I peaked outside my window another dimension of rhythm emerged. Rigid foothills and wild slopes *disturbed* unwrinkled territory. Barren deserts transitioned into lush forests. Colossal mountain peaks packed with glaciers *dominated* an area notorious for wildfires. I witnessed the Cascade Mountains for the very first time. Miles and miles of *untouched* land stretched beyond my imagination. Evergreens towered against a heavenly sky.

Once the plane completed a final turn, Puget Sound slowly appeared. Moments later, *I gaped in complete amazement* at Seattle's skyline. Having a new home *invigorated* me. Five years after my bullying incident—*I was no longer chained to past mistakes.*

--

Seattle's hilly topography and public transit reminded me of San Francisco. I deeply appreciated the fact Seattle enjoyed a fairly large middle-class presence—when I first lived there housing was reasonable priced. The Emerald City seemed like a great place to launch a career and raise a family. In addition, I really valued the fact Seattle was not too large in terms of population and land area.

Although Seattle is notorious for its rain, I saw nothing but sunshine. During the late afternoon, the temperature peaked in the mid-70s. Unlike most states along the eastern seaboard,

Washington's climate is more arid. In fact, Washington is the second largest wine producing state (only behind California). Between May and October, Western Washington's climate is identical to Northern California. Although some mornings start off with light mist (known as June Gloom), the sun typically burns out any remaining fog before lunchtime.

One reason I loved Seattle was that I didn't need a car. Students and faculty at University of Washington receive ten weeks of unlimited public transit access each quarter. I used this opportunity to travel across the region on countless adventures.

Kicked Out of Microsoft Headquarters

While sitting in my urban planning class, one student expressed how residents of Bellevue frequently menace the city's homeless population. Since my bullying incident in high school, I didn't believe that *any* city in King County was *less tolerant* than my hometown. In order to prove that student's premise was inaccurate, I whimsically traveled to Bellevue with just my backpack, a little money, and a few snacks. Although I usually plan each hour of my day—this trip had no specific pathway. During this mission I wanted to know if Bellevue was really hostile towards vagrants. I not only rode a bus to somewhere I've never been, but I didn't notify anyone what I was doing.

Once my bus crossed Lake Washington I wasn't sure where to get off. The first stop was a commuter parking lot (adjacent to Interstate 405). Since nothing was there I continued riding. After driving past expensive houses I arrived at Bellevue Square, an indoor shopping mall. My friend in landscape architecture worked at Crate and Barrel so I went inside to see if she was working. I did my best to blend in by window-shopping through several luxury stores. It was really cool being able to blend with the local crowd. Even though I've never been to Bellevue—I felt more at home.

I was a vagrant college student who just started a new life. As I stepped outside Bellevue Square, I walked to the nearest Starbucks to get something to eat. Once I left, I journeyed one block east to a nearby pocket park (across from the city's transit center). Even though I was in the heart of downtown—nobody was there on Saturday afternoon.

During first quarter, my landscape architecture instructor took *many* breaks. It was not uncommon for her to step outside for ten minutes while students were completing projects. She frequently claimed, *"I need to put money in the parking meter."* Even when students weren't working on projects, she would schedule "bathroom breaks" (which lasted ten minutes). My friend and I both thought she creatively conjured ways to take smoking breaks. Since studio lasted for nearly four hours, it was difficult for my instructor to survive the entire class without enjoying a cigarette break.

While I was at the Bellevue Transit Center I decided to take a "smoking break." I ripped a piece of paper from my notebook and used it to roll a fake joint. I grabbed moss and pulled grass to create makeshift cannabis. Since it rained earlier in the day, the grass and dirt caused my filter to moisten. As a result, I experienced more difficulty assembling this cigarette. Once I delicately taped each side of the filter and tightened the blend, I blew into an unfastened mouthpiece. A nauseating mix of grass and mud came spewing out. A clean sidewalk was tainted by a heap of sludge.

After my smoking break, I snuck into Microsoft Headquarters. I went inside the Center City building because I wanted to show my friends *how* I snuck into a corporate office. My objective was to take the elevator to the 26th floor and capture photos of the entire process. Just before I reached the elevator, a police officer approached me and sternly asked, *"Where's your ID? Show me your badge!"*

Before I could formulate a rational response—I ran outside to avoid arrest. As I was fleeing Microsoft Headquarters I clung to my backpack to assure nothing fell out. Although I was never charged with trespassing, I finally recognized Bellevue was in fact more hostile towards vagrants than I initially imagined.

As soon as I dashed across a busy street, I slowly walked back to the Bellevue Transit Center. I sat a picnic table and called Marianne DiStefano (who is my Aunt and Godmother). Marianne was staying in Florida at the time. I called her to notify how a homeless fact finding trip involved me getting kicked out of Microsoft Headquarters and rolling a fake joint. As the sun began to set against the Olympic Mountains, Marianne told me she had to leave. Before I hung up, I told Marianne, "I can't wait to see you again someday!" Once my conversation ended I hopped on a bus and ventured back home.

Lost in Ballard

My roommate in college was an avid runner. He frequently ran along a five-mile stretch of the Burke-Gilman Trail from his dorm to the Ballard Locks. Although I was never a runner, I was eager to see where the Burke-Gilman Trail ended. One dreary morning I decided to embark on another whimsical expedition. This time I was going to visit the Ballard Locks (with only a backpack and bottle of water). Throughout my class, students raved about Ballard. Since I never went there, I decided to go one weekend. My four-mile quest along the Burke-Gilman Trail began outside my dorm.

During this rainy morning low clouds were releasing small circuits of mist. Although I did not need a raincoat, I could feel my clothes conjoin to the morning dew. As I walked underneath the giant Ship Canal Bridge (which carries twelve lanes of Interstate 5) I crossed into the Wallingford neighborhood. While I was walking several bikers raced past me, in some cases I was never warned as they approached. On one occasion I almost *crashed* into one biker. Despite almost being involved in a serious accident, I did not let fear stifle my exploration.

The first landmark I encountered during this journey was Gas Works Park. This site is situated along the bend of Lake Union. Gas Works Park has breathtaking views of downtown. The first time I went to this park was during my landscape architecture class. Although traversing through this familiar and iconic park was impressive, I had to walk even further to step outside my comfort zone.

The Burke-Gilman Trail is relatively fragmented because it traverses through a series of diverse landscapes across North Seattle. My trip along this path involved me crossing through parks, busy streets, alleyways, and even the parking lot of a local shipyard. As I walked further west I could see my destination across the vista. There was a giant cantilever steel bridge that crossed over the Lake Washington Ship Canal. As a human I felt *overwhelmed* by the scale of this structure because it stood 167 feet above the ground and stretched for almost 3,000 feet.

Once I walked underneath this bridge I was *certain* that I would reach the Ballard Locks, however a concrete monster crossed my path. It was the Fremont Troll. In 1990 local artists decided to construct an 18-foot public sculpture beneath the Aurora Bridge. I initially thought the Fremont Troll originated from the earth's bedrock, however it was constructed using concrete and steel. This monument is an iconic element of Seattle because it symbolizes Fremont's culture of public art. Although I was not at the Ballard Locks, I was highly impressed by this whimsical experience.

Fremont is a trendy area. In recent years, housing costs have rapidly increased. Fremont is home to many high tech companies such as Adobe and Google. As I walked past Google's office I decided *not* to sneak into their headquarters because I didn't want to get kicked out of another corporate office.

As the Aurora Bridge faded into the distance, I was no longer inside my comfort zone. Gas Works Park and downtown were both out of sight.

Ralph Waldo Emerson wrote a famous quote, *"Do not go where the path may lead, go instead where there is no path and leave a trail."* Once I reached the intersection of NW 43rd Street and 8th Avenue NW the Burke-Gilman Trail unexpectedly ended. Since I wasn't familiar with this area, I faced a very tough decision. There were no signs and continuing along the main path wouldn't lead me anywhere.

The first option involved retracting my entire walk. I didn't want to return to campus because there were no public restrooms (on my way back). During this time, I *really* had to use the bathroom. I couldn't walk another three miles before making a pit stop.

After going back and forth, I ultimately continued walking west towards Ballard. I diverted onto Leary Way NW. Although this street crosses through several single-family residential communities, it's a major arterial road in Northwest Seattle. During this time I did my best to walk towards areas with high concentrations of commercial and retail activity. As soon as I saw signs for Fred Meyer and Trader Joe's, I recognized that I was in an urban environment. I used physical features to assist me throughout this journey. Despite being lost, I was not fearful that morning. If I had the strength to overcome a gruesome bullying incident in high school, I was *determined* to find my way 3,000 miles from home.

Life is about overcoming a series of complex challenges. I used this experience to not only step outside my comfort zone, but take command of my mind and soul. I was not going to react to something that didn't exist. It's easy for humans to panic over ambiguity because it prevents them from formulating a future plan. When I was lost in Ballard I was not concerned about my future, my focus was centered on the present, which meant getting home safely. What gave me the strength of will and strength of emotion that morning was reminding myself, "I'm in a better place *now* than where I was during high school." Being lost in Ballard allowed me to remove myself from reality and solve my own obstacles.

As I approached Fred Meyer I went inside because I needed to use the restroom. Once I left the bathroom, I grabbed a shopping basket and pretended to briefly shop for groceries. I did not want any employees to realize I was using this place as a pit stop.

Shortly after leaving Fred Meyer I continued walking west along Leary Way NW. When I finally arrived in Ballard, I came across several car repair shops, hardware stores, public storage facilities, and shipyards. This neighborhood was *not* the romantic place I initially envisioned.

The Ballard Bridge is an elevated drawbridge that crosses Salmon Bay. It carries traffic along 15th Avenue NW. Many buses are routed through this bridge because it connects Ballard to several neighborhoods. Shortly after approaching this rustic structure I saw something I was waiting for. It was a bus stop—my ticket home. I sprinted to the bus stop to find out which buses traveled through this area. As I *wheezed* for oxygen I saw the 29 bus route listed. This route connects Ballard to downtown Seattle. Instead of walking another four miles to my dorm, I decided to ride a bus to downtown and connect onto another bus to the University District.

I was really thankful once I realized that I would be able to get home *on my own*. Even though I ventured outside my comfort zone for quite a long time, I was ready to get back to campus because I was *hungry*. I spent the next several minutes waiting at the bus stop. As I looked into the distance my patience *finally* paid off.

7 DREAMS AND LEADERSHIP

"I like to be a free spirit. Some don't like that, but that's the way I am."
-Diana Princess of Wales

September 28, 2011 marked my first day as a full-time matriculated student at the University of Washington. After years of hard work I finally enrolled in one of the top performing universities in the country. My high school guidance counselor was *astonished* once he learned this news. Shortly after entering the Community, Environment, and Planning (CEP) program I reached out to Emily Janes, Sarah Showalter, and Christine Wenzel. I thanked each of them for helping me attain my dream. I was also eager to discuss how I managed to secure a fantastic internship and find a great home. Furthermore, I noted that attending the University of Washington was the *best* risk I ever pursued.

The Community, Environment, and Planning (CEP) program has shaped my values. This program truly offers undergraduates an enriching experience. My favorite part about CEP was the fact it incorporates a lot of social activities. Shortly after leaving Connecticut it was difficult for me to form friendships—CEP provided me several opportunities to socialize with fellow students. In some cases, casual conversations evolved into close relationships.

The Senior Project is the cornerstone of CEP. Each student is required to complete an intensive capstone, which could encompass any topic related to a student's interest. When I first entered college I decided that I was going to concentrate on urban design.

Senior Project: Building an Inclusive Community

During my first quarter I enrolled in a class called CEP 200: Introduction to Community, Environment, and Planning. Students in this seminar are required to participate in an outside service learning activity. While researching potential internships, I was fortunate to find a place that matched my interests. After reviewing an online database, I came across a nonprofit organization called University Heights Community Center Association.

During my first day I rode the bus to an old elementary school. When I first walked in it reminded me of a place I frequently volunteered at during high school. University Heights emulated a similar atmosphere to the Green Street Arts Center in Middletown, Connecticut. My first impression of University Heights was that it was slightly unkempt, artsy, and serviced mostly low-income families. When I first walked through the main entrance I noticed chipped paint across the building's exterior. Despite having a lackluster first impression of this building, I would spend the next three years interning at this special organization. The people who worked there would help advance my fight for others. I eventually realized beneath the surface, this building offered more opportunities than I could possibly imagine.

Shortly after entering the main office I spoke with Dorothy Lengyel, the organization's Executive Director. The best way I could initially describe Dorothy was that her leadership style was creative and firm. During our first conversation Dorothy asked, "What's your interests…what are you looking for in an internship?"

Once I mentioned landscape architecture—something clicked. Little did I know; her organization was looking for a new intern to help facilitate the construction and design of a new playground for students with learning disabilities. By the end of this discussion, Dorothy believed my experience would benefit her organization.

Interning at University Heights not only helped fulfill an important graduation requirement, but it allowed me to connect with a prominent leader in Seattle's gay community.

Three Words: 43rd District Democrats

Jamie Pedersen was first elected to the Washington House of Representatives in 2006. He represents the 43rd district, which covers downtown and several surrounding neighborhoods. In 2005 he served with Lambda Legal as the lead attorney in *Andersen v. King County*. This lawsuit sought to overturn the state's ban on same-sex marriage. In 2009 he authored Washington's "everything but marriage" law. This provision expanded 300 new benefits to same-sex couples.

During my internship at University Heights, I caught sight of something I thought was too good to be true. *Three words* led me towards a dark corner office. Once I entered this mysterious room, I spoke with a young woman named Katy Buck. I casually asked, "What office is this?"

She responded by saying, "Hi, my name is Katy. I'm the Legislative Aide for State Representative Jamie Pedersen. This office houses legislative members from the 43rd District."

I felt a mix of intimidation and excitement. Growing up I struggled to find gay men in politics. Although I was not a visible leader during my fight for the School Violence Prevention Act, I did my best to represent the values and interests for the gay community at-large. While speaking with Katy I discussed the time I helped shepherd the School Violence Prevention Act. In addition, I mentioned the time I fought back against attempts to outlaw same-sex marriage in the Connecticut Constitution.

Towards the end of this conversation I told her; "Tell Jamie I want to *thank* him for advancing the rights of gays and lesbians!"

Before I left, Katy handed me a scrap piece of paper. She assured whatever I wrote would be shared directly with Representative Pedersen. I took advantage of this special moment to thank my political idol for his remarkable leadership:

> "*You are such an inspiration.* I am so proud of your hard work for the gay community. You are an incredible individual!"

Although I wrote a personal message to Representative Pedersen, I wondered if I would ever meet him face to face.

Katy asked, "Do you ever see yourself running for public office?" In a nonchalant manner I replied, "No, I don't plan on running for office. *I won't get elected.* Besides I'm pursuing a career in urban design…"

Right before I walked away Katy mentioned, "I think you'd make a *great* leader. We *need* more gay men in politics. Your experience forging a bi-partisan coalition in the North Carolina legislature at such a young age is deeply impressive!"

Financial Challenges

Well before I started college, my family faced numerous financial challenges. My mother worked as a teacher, and didn't get paid during the summer months. As a result, my father managed to work extra shifts at his job just so our family could make ends meet. When I was in high school, my family's expenses increased significantly. My parents were not well equipped when it came to avoiding financial impulsivity or tracking household spending.

Although my mom is very organized, her spending habits are highly fanciful. Her decisions are very impulsive especially when it comes to purchasing expensive items. I was the one in my family who advised her to *wait* 48 hours before making a major purchase. My mother's biggest weakness was that it took her a very long time to understand scarcity.

My father on the other hand is more practical, however his organization and internal strategy skills are very deficient. My dad is not a fan of deadlines and he values a work in progress over a finished product. Even though I have a great relationship with my father, he is not outgoing.

Although I was initially ecstatic to transfer to University of Washington, I wasn't sure if my parents were positioned to provide *any* financial support. I never expected my parents to cover the entire cost of my education, however I wanted them to supplement the offset that was not covered by personal savings and financial aid.

Before I left UConn in 2010 I met with Rachel Brock, a financial aid advisor. She helped me formulate a game plan so that I could not only participate in the National Student Exchange, but acquire enough student loans to fund my first quarter at University of Washington. In April 2010 I decided to use $6,500 of student loans from UConn to pay for my junior year at University of Washington. In addition, financial aid counselors helped secure an additional $12,500 in student loans. I also had to take out a $2,500 short-term loan from the financial aid office. When I combined my personal savings and student loans I had allocated $23,500.

Despite securing $23,500 just to pay for my third year of college, I faced a $4,500 shortfall. If I couldn't eliminate this deficit, I would be forced to drop out of school. To make matters worse, I witnessed several of my fellow colleagues withdraw from the university because they couldn't keep up with ongoing tuition hikes. My worst fear was being next.

Life Review

I was standing by myself in the middle of a tall coniferous forest. During this early October afternoon I walked alone on a private trail (which stretched a half-mile). I had no map and could not see beyond my immediate surroundings. This landscape stretched beyond my imagination. The Evergreen trees were so expansive— they blocked my eyesight. Despite positioning my eye towards the future, my objective was focused on the present. This forest did not allow me to determine my own fate; I could only use my past experience to strive towards a better tomorrow.

As I embarked on this walk I used this moment as a life review. The best way to describe a life review is to imagine watching your life history unfold in chronological sequence and in extreme detail. Imagine being videotaped since the day you were born and seeing every precious moment of your life flash before your eyes. Think about how a single event impacts your life; try to imagine how *one* decision changed your life (over a five or ten year period) because of subsequent actions that followed.

The best way to describe my life review was that it combined past, present, and future memories into a single experience. In addition, this experience helped me understand why people *thrive* or *decline* over a long period of time.

Prior to this journey I thought about death as it pertained to others, but I never thought about my own. The closest time I encountered death was on November 3, 2005. There were several reasons I attempted to take my own life. During that afternoon I received several threats at school. In addition, my sexual orientation was leaked to the entire student body. Aside from feeling rejected, the biggest factor that contributed to this decision was the fact I felt *alone* and *trapped* inside my hometown.

Once I swallowed an entire bottle of anti-depressants—I was convinced my hours were numbered. My suicide attempt occurred in the late evening. I remember crying hysterically and checking the clock because I wanted to leave.

Before I went to bed I figured that I would die in my sleep and see total darkness. After the worst day of my life I went to bed prepared for nightmares. Even though my day at school was horrific, I fell asleep feeling a real sense of peace. Whether it was spiritual or medicinal—I saw whiteness all around me. It was more beautiful and comforting than anyone I had ever loved. This love was so immeasurable: I could remain single for the rest of my life and feel universal acceptance.

On the following morning I woke up in complete amazement. Even though I had every reason to feel lots of pain for having so many drugs inside my body—I didn't. For just a few seconds, I forgot about *all* my past mistakes because I realized God knows each of us and loves us more than we could possibly imagine.

Towards the end of my life review I encountered another whiteness. Several yards away stood a mysterious opening. This threshold was the point of no return. A narrow dirt path opened into an immense field. Towering trees transitioned to short grass. A masked sky suddenly unleashed every mystery—I made it to Mac's Pond.

Cheerful birds were singing. The sound of chirps rivaled the same melody as John Lennon's song "Imagine." Being on Bainbridge Island allowed me to return to my childhood innocence because I didn't feel any pain. I felt connected to nature in a way I never experienced. Frogs, birds, and ducks shared one space in complete harmony. This was nature at its best.

Even though I was by myself, I felt oneness with everything. Walking on this path empowered me to seek unity within my heart and mind. After my life review I realized there was a place on this Earth where I belonged. As I looked up, I thought about the moment I attempted suicide. Had I ended my life I wouldn't enjoy any opportunities to love, learn, and grow into the person I am today. I realized that God not only knows and loves me, but he has a secret plan for my life that is full of hope.

Final Wish

After undergoing an intense life review, Caitlin Dean, my undergraduate advisor scheduled a meeting with all her students. She asked each student to rip a scrap piece of paper and write down three goals for next year.

When I wrote my three goals I asked for three basic wishes. I wanted to see health and wholeness within myself and loved ones. In addition, I wrote that I hope my personal finances *do not* derail my education.

Once I finished writing my three wishes, I folded this piece of paper *really tightly* and handed it to Caitlin. Although my fate was extremely uncertain, the future had yet to be written.

Mary Gates Leadership Scholarship

Towards the end of autumn, Caitlin Dean sent an e-mail to all her students because the application period for the Mary Gates Scholarship officially opened. At first, I felt very skeptical (because I didn't think I would ever win). Throughout college and high school I applied for several scholarships and typically *never* heard a response.

During this school year, most of my time was divided between studying, interning, and searching for employment. As I *endlessly* searched for additional financial aid, I went online to view the Mary Gates Endowment program.

The Mary Gates Endowment was established in 1995 through a $10 million dollar donation from Bill and Melinda Gates. Four years later, the University of Washington received an additional $10 million from the Gates family to expand this program. Since then, this fund has grown into one of the largest endowments at the university—all proceeds are dedicated exclusively to undergraduates.

When I was a student, the Mary Gates Endowment offered either a research or leadership scholarship. I first examined the research scholarship because I thought it was most in line with my Senior Project.

The Mary Gates Research Scholarship is highly competitive. Students are required to document tangible research by writing a paper that includes scientific charts and interviews. Research applicants are *required* to secure a mentor who serves as a faculty member. This requisite precluded me from competing for this scholarship because Dorothy Lengyel was not a faculty member.

The Mary Gates Leadership Scholarship was *slightly* less rigorous because it only required applicants to write a 1,200-word essay, create a project title, and secure a mentor (who didn't have to be a faculty member). As I reviewed each of the application prerequisites—I began to formulate a game plan. At that moment, I realized my Senior Project was on a comparable track to other leadership applicants. Once I realized I had a fighting chance, I was no longer afraid to pursue this opportunity.

Most students spend Winter Break catching up with old friends and relaxing, however I was fighting to continue my education. When I was in Connecticut, I spent much of my time preparing my application and formulating written arguments for the Mary Gates Leadership Scholarship. In my essay I discussed how I helped facilitate the design and construction of a new playground. Additionally, I expressed how this playground was geared towards meeting the needs of students with learning disabilities.

Shortly after submitting my application, I was offered an interview. On the day before my meeting, Dorothy advised: "Stay optimistic. I'll be thinking positive thoughts while you have your interview tomorrow morning. NO POLITICS."

My interview was scheduled on a cold rainy morning. While waiting in the front office, I realized I was already in a better place compared to seven years ago. Before I knew it, a young woman walked in and asked who I was. I responded by shaking her hand and saying, "Hi, my name is Gabe Filer. I'm here for the interview with the Mary Gates Endowment committee."

Moments later she directed me towards a secluded office. Four staff members walked in and each introduced themselves. At the start of this interview, one reviewer noted, "This meeting is *not* a formal interview. The purpose of this conversation is for us to get to know you, and for you to explain your project. Don't be intimidated by this process."

During the first question I was asked, "Tell us about your yourself...what is your personal background?"

"My name is Gabriel Filer and I'm a junior studying

Community, Environment, and Planning. In 2010 I began interning at the University Heights Community Center Association. My objective was to assist the organization design a new playground for students with learning disabilities. When I was three years old I was diagnosed with autism…I couldn't read, write, or even compile a sentence…"

As I revealed sensitive information, I could hear each panelist jotting down extensive notes. Aside from my voice—the only audible thing in that room was the sound of pen ink racing across four small notepads.

Shortly after, I was asked my next question. During this time, I reached a critical crossroads when one reviewer asked: "What is your definition of leadership and how has it applied to your academic career?"

"In 2009 I teamed with North Carolina State Senator Julia Boseman to help pass the School Violence Prevention Act. For nearly three years Senator Boseman has introduced SB 526. Each time she has introduced this measure Republicans blocked it in the state legislature.

In 2008 my home state legalized same-sex marriage. Shortly after the 2008 election I decided to enter politics because I wanted to spread the same hope I was fortunate to receive at such a young age. In less than a month, I contacted over sixty lawmakers and organizations and campaigned for gay rights nationwide.

On June 30, 2009 North Carolina became the ninth state to enact a comprehensive anti-bullying law. Two days before my high school graduation I helped advance legislative history. This provision was not only the first piece of gay rights legislation under Governor Perdue's Administration, but I managed to break a forty-year legislative impasse.

Leadership is *not* about a title—it's about the people you *never* hear from that are fighting each day to make the world a better place. *Anyone* can be a leader…even if you come from nothing."

Once I recited this audacious response, Dorothy's voice *screamed*, "NO POLITICS" inside my head. Despite the fact I was urged to *not* mention politics, I determined it was best to separate myself from other applicants. Well before my interview, I realized the benefit of covering politics greatly outweighed any risks.

A few weeks later, one of my three wishes came true—I was awarded the Mary Gates Leadership Scholarship. Winning this scholarship was *not* the end, but rather a new beginning towards my fight for justice, equality, and human dignity.

8 SAME-SEX MARRIAGE IN WASHINGTON

"Without people challenging how things are and aspiring for things to be better, how would progress ever happen."
-Christine Wenzel

Once North Carolina enacted the School Violence Prevention Act, I never considered re-entering politics. Towards the end of 2011 I met with Katy Buck, the Legislative Aide for State Representative Jamie Pedersen. Katy and I enjoyed frequent conversations since her office was located at University Heights.

During our conversation she informed me that lawmakers were hoping to pass a same-sex marriage bill during this upcoming legislative session. In addition, she revealed that Democrats in the House of Representatives already found someone to sponsor this bill. Just before I left, Katy mentioned, "Same-sex marriage is one of the top three priorities on the legislative agenda for 2012. The other two priorities for Democrats are creating jobs and cutting government spending."

Shortly after my conversation with Katy, I heard another call to go forth and help others because I needed to help proponents of same-sex marriage overcome another legislative obstacle. Just before Christmas break I was doing something I did three years ago—I was contacting state lawmakers and organizing another legislative effort to make history. I reached out to several State Senators in Washington and *urged* them to support same-sex marriage.

Once 2012 arrived my work to not only pass a same-sex marriage bill, but a potential statewide referendum began. Christine Wenzel once told me, "Without people challenging how things are and aspiring for things to be better, how would progress ever happen." I was determined to use each day I lived to fight just as hard as I did in North Carolina. In the days following the New Year I signed a petition launched by the Chair of the Washington State Democratic Party. This petition was sponsored by the grassroots organization Washington United for Marriage.

New Friendships and Political Opportunities

The first time I met Claire Mueller was when we both were working on a climate change project in class. We were both assigned to a group that had to facilitate a lecture on how the media frames climate change. During one meeting we both exchanged ideas. After a terse conversation she sent me an e-mail thanking me for my hard work in class. In her message she stated, "I just wanted to say *thanks* for being *awesome*, and keep being the *awesome you* that *you* are!" Reading that message marked the beginning of my friendship with her because it provided me the comfort I needed for me to share my story.

A defining moment of our friendship occurred on February 10, 2012. During that Friday morning, I approached Claire after class. In a casual voice I asked, "What are your thoughts on gay marriage, do you like the fact the legislature is addressing this matter?" In a cheerful voice she mentioned; "I *strongly* support marriage equality...I'm *really* happy our state is finally moving in that direction!" Once Claire expressed her support, I revealed the moment I became a gay rights activist. In addition, I informed her about the time I campaigned for same-sex marriage in Connecticut. Claire was not only astonished to learn about my activism, but my inner life caught her by surprise.

During that afternoon, I e-mailed Claire a copy of my written testimony for the School Violence Prevention Act. I shared this story because I believed she would respond warmly. Once she read my blog, she expressed:

"I am awed by what you've gone through and I think

> the work you've done is really cool. I think we're all
> really lucky to be in a class with someone who has such
> a strong dedication to equality and respect for all."

Shortly after reading her e-mail, I elaborated in great detail about the time the Connecticut Supreme Court legalized same-sex marriage and how voters defeated a Constitutional Convention. Additionally, I mentioned how same-sex marriage received bi-partisan support in the Connecticut Assembly. In April 2009, State Senator Beth Bye introduced SB 899, this updated Connecticut's marriage laws with genderless language. In addition, it codified the *Kerrigan v. Commissioner of Public Health* ruling. This bill passed the Connecticut House of Representatives (by a vote of 100-44) and the Connecticut Senate (by a vote of 28-7). Half of the Republican State Senators voted in favor of SB 899. Governor Rell signed this measure on April 23, 2009. I shared this story with Claire because I wanted her to believe what happened in Connecticut could someday occur in Washington.

On February 1, 2012 SB 6239 (which legalized same-sex marriage in Washington) passed the State Senate in by a vote of 28-21. Gay rights activists hailed this moment because same-sex marriage cleared its largest legislative hurdle. On February 8 the House of Representatives passed SB 6239 by a margin of 55-43. Governor Christine Gregoire was instrumental when it came to shepherding this policy. Earlier that month, I thanked the Governor for advocating this important issue.

On February 13, 2012 I could hardly pay attention during class. That afternoon Governor Gregoire held a bill signing ceremony for SB 6239 in the Washington State Capitol. This event was open to several media outlets and members of the public. Although I was unable to attend this important event, I was elated that Washington became the seventh state to permit same-sex marriage. During that afternoon I thought about the time Connecticut legalized same-sex marriage. The same excitement I felt in Connecticut three years ago was recurring in Washington. Before signing SB 6239 into law Governor Gregoire delivered an impassioned speech on the issue of marriage equality. She told reporters at a crowded press conference:

> "Isn't it time for this state to send a message *all across the world* we in this state stand proudly for *equality*. If

asked those questions with their *heads* and their *hearts* I
believe the people of the State of Washington will say,
"Yes." Marriage Equality is right for our state and our
time is *now*, the time is *today."*

Shortly after delivering a powerful speech, the halls inside the
Washington State Capitol ignited with jubilation. Once Governor
Gregoire signed SB 6239 into law, I was amazed to watch this issue
result from impassioned citizens instead of a court fight. The
legislature sent a same-sex marriage bill to the Governor's desk
because enough people in Washington believed in what's possible.
Dreams and possibilities emerge from the human imagination,
innovation does not stem from reality. Monumental
accomplishments mankind has achieved such as implementing
universal healthcare in fifty-eights nations and abolishing capital
punishment in ninety-eight countries demonstrates the importance
of embracing a vivid imagination.

SB 6239 was so remarkable because Washington became the
first (and only) western state to legalize same-sex marriage.
Whenever I examined a map of states that enacted gay marriage,
there was a stark political contrast between Washington and
neighboring states. The closest jurisdiction in the United States that
recognized or performed any marriages between same-sex couples
was Iowa. Although Washington stood out, it was not because this
state suddenly transformed into a "sore-thumb."

As the geography of states permitting same-sex marriage
underwent a major expansion in 2012, it reminded me of the time
when Massachusetts and Connecticut were the only two states
featured on this map. When I was in middle school I was told
Connecticut would become a "nation embarrassment" for passing
civil unions, however this map reiterates the importance of *standing
out* and being on the right side of history. It's crucial for states to
not follow political trends, but *pioneer* social movements and extend
opportunities.

The issue of same-sex marriage is not just about weddings—it's
about extending hope. Opportunities occur when someone takes a
chance on someone else. At this moment, I realized that
Washington was not only taking a chance on me, but countless
people who wanted to live their life like everyone else. I was
gratified that someone believed in me and understood that I should

not be forced to board a six-hour flight just to marry someone I loved. I deeply appreciated that Washington did not wait for the United States Supreme Court or the federal government before moving forward on this important issue.

Later that evening, my parents called me from Connecticut. They told me that they watched Governor Gregoire sign SB 6239 into law. I informed them that even though a marriage bill was signed, it could be repealed because Washington law permits voters to overturn legislative policies through initiatives and referendums.

Referendum 74: The Campaign Begins

Less than four hours after Governor Gregoire signed SB 6239 into law, opponents launched a fierce campaign to dismantle same-sex marriage. Conservatives were determined to put the rights of same-sex couples on the ballot (just like they did in Connecticut and California). Preserve Marriage Washington organized a brutal campaign and submitted over 200,000 signatures to the Secretary of State's office. On June 12, 2012 the Washington Secretary of State announced that Referendum 74 would appear on the November ballot after undergoing a random check of signatures.

As soon as same-sex marriage cleared the State Senate, I started organizing. Since the beginning of the year, I knew 2012 would be a very exhaustive campaign cycle. I used my college campus to organize a large voting block. Prior to the passage of SB 6239, I helped my co-worker register to vote. In addition, I tried convincing members of the University Senate to approve a resolution expressing support for Referendum 74. I also teamed with Claire Mueller to do a gay rights speech in front of a group of students at the University of Washington. During my speech I said; "When Joe Biden expressed his support for same-sex marriage, it came from his *heart*. I hope that you will vote from your *heart* and approve Referendum 74!"

Meeting My Political Hero

April 17, 2012 was a moment of consequence. I spent several hours finalizing important deadlines for my Senior Project. By the end of the day, I couldn't even focus. As I gazed into the distance, I was slapped with a great surprise. In just a few hours Jamie Pedersen was scheduled to host a Town Hall Meeting at University Heights. Once I learned the co-sponsor of same-sex marriage was going to be upstairs, I erupted with excitement because I finally had the opportunity to meet someone I deeply admired.

As I was celebrating (outside Dorothy's office), my honeymoon came to a screeching halt. During the past several months I was doubtful that I would *ever* meet Representative Pedersen. Whenever I spoke with his Legislative Aide I acquired an impression he was always busy. As a result, I never believed he would visit the organization I interned while I was there. I felt more anxious after each minute because I never thought how "I would" approach my hero. I use the term "I would" because it's very circumstantial.

Circumstances force tough decisions. Before I could contemplate the best method to introduce myself, Jamie Pedersen walked past my office. A narrow window of opportunity just opened and there was little time to think. Within five minutes, I quietly walked upstairs with my digital camera. I sneaked into a large auditorium, and saw a handsome blonde man. Although most politicians wear expensive suits and sport a sophisticated necktie, this individual was casually dressed. He wore a gray sweater vest and sage windbreaker.

Before I introduced myself I tactfully asked, "Are *you* Jamie Pedersen?" Once he answered, I thanked him for his dedication to advancing the rights of gays and lesbians. I took advantage of this opportunity to discuss the time I championed the School Violence Prevention Act. In addition, I commended him for crafting the state's same-sex marriage bill. Although he was fearful voters could repeal this measure, I assured him that I've fought for same-sex marriage across the country.

Representative Pedersen was speechless when he learned the depth of my political activism. What caught him by surprise was the fact I was a silent leader. His facial expression revealed how impressive it is for somebody to accomplish political victories while remaining anonymous. Leadership is *not* about a job title, what counts most are the invisible advocates fighting on the front lines each day. Just before I left, I had my picture taken with Jamie because I never wanted to forget that experience.

Shortly after arriving home, I e-mailed Claire a copy of my photo with Jamie Pedersen. In addition, I explained; "Jamie expressed fear that voters might repeal the gay marriage law." A few hours later Claire responded, "It *won't* get repealed, cause there are too many Washingtonians who understand the power of *love*!" Claire's compassion towards helping others was extremely evident throughout this campaign. She and I both teamed during several occasions to ensure Washington would someday join Connecticut.

Fundraising for Same-Sex Marriage

On July 21, 2012 I stepped outside to another gorgeous morning in Western Washington. The air was crisp, and a gentle breeze cooled my body as I walked though the University District. I bubbled with enthusiasm because I was going to visit my best friend. I had not seen Claire Mueller in over a month; I was extremely eager to catch up. Earlier we agreed to meet for breakfast. Before I flew back to Connecticut, she invited me to the Block Party Throwdown, a fundraiser being sponsored by Washington United for Marriage. This organization was hosting a dodgeball tournament in Seattle's Capitol Hill neighborhood to raise money for Referendum 74.

As I approached the bus stop, I sprinted just before it left. At the last minute I caught the driver's attention and *pleaded* him to let me in. Fortunately this driver was sympathetic because he opened the door. As I struggled to pull change out of my pocket I gasped for oxygen.

Once I arrived in Capitol Hill, I was dropped off in front of Saint Mark's Cathedral. Claire told me she lived nearby, however I couldn't find her. After sending her several text messages, she told me to walk south as if I were heading towards Broadway. As I walked past many expensive homes I saw a group of people jumping up and down in the far distance. I said to myself, "Who are those *maniacs*, are they a bunch of protesters who want America to withdraw from the United Nations?" As I walked closer and closer to the corner of East Roy and 10th Avenue I realized that it was Claire and her husband Archie Sherwood. Once I detected them—I ran as fast as I could because I was thrilled to reunite with them.

My body leaped with excitement as I shouted (in the most high pitch voice), "*Claire*...how are *you*! I missed *you* so much!" I greeted her with the tightest and longest-lasting hug I could remember because we were both teaming up once again to help advance same-sex marriage. Once I managed to control my emotions I walked with her and Archie to a small restaurant on Broadway to eat breakfast. For the next two hours we caught up and enjoyed each other's company.

At 12:00 pm the Block Party Throwdown was scheduled to begin. The members of my team included Claire, Archie, and some of his friends from the electrical engineering department. During that afternoon, the temperature peaked in the high-70s. Before I entered the court I was sweating like a pig. This was the first time I stepped foot inside a dodgeball court since middle school.

During our first game one individual shouted incredibly pervasive remarks towards my team. His name was Alex Broner. He was a twenty-seven-year-old graduate student studying at the University of Hawaii. At first Alex was extremely rude. He didn't hesitate to yell crude statements if someone struck out (or was ever injured). When someone was hit directly in the face with a curve ball he laughed loudly.

Even though I was forced to compete against him, this wasn't the first time I encountered a bully. Alex practiced dodgeball each day at Cal Anderson Park. For some reason I had a feeling that he conditioned himself for quite some time. My instinct proved to be true. During this round our team was slaughtered. Whenever someone tried to grab the ball everyone (from the opposing team) fired cannons. Before I knew it, we lost.

As I left the dodgeball court I did my best to maintain a positive spirit. Although I was disappointed that our team was eliminated during the first round, I was really happy to spend the entire afternoon with Claire and Archie. During the rest of the afternoon we talked about the upcoming election and discussed what we believed would happen. I also told Claire I will be flying to Connecticut before the end of the month.

Just before the winners were announced, Washington United for Marriage delivered several boxes of cheese and pepperoni pizza. Even though my team came in dead last we were the first one to get our hands on the warm boxes of pizza. Claire, Archie, and I secretly each grabbed three slices before running off. Although we did not win the tournament, we at least secured a free meal before anyone else.

As we walked outside the park, I joked at how we are going to look back at this silly afternoon several years from now. The Block Party Throwdown fundraiser was a major success. This event enjoyed over sixty participants and raised $1,400 for the Referendum 74 campaign.

As I briefly glanced over another scenic sunset in Western Washington, Archie pulled Claire aside and whispered, "We *need* to head home now." Even though I was surprised to learn my evening with them was being cut short, I was gratified that I had the opportunity to catch up with Claire. The final words I shouted to Claire as she was being pulled away by Archie were, *"I'll be thinking of you when I'm in Connecticut!"*

Election Day: Living on Edge

I was living the Question 1 campaign all over again. Over the past nine months supporters and opponents of same-sex marriage spent millions of dollars trying to influence voters in Washington. Referendum 74 generated a large number of individual donors (which almost matched the record set in 2008 when voters approved Initiative 1000).

By October 5, 2012, Washington United for Marriage raised $9.4 million in political donations while Preserve Marriage Washington raised roughly $1 million. Proponents of same-sex marriage enjoyed a major fundraising advantage and received endorsements by several corporations, newspapers, and elected officials. The business community in Washington was incredibly influential when it came to funding the Referendum 74 war chest. Amazon.com CEO Jeff Bezos and his wife pledged $2.5 million and Microsoft co-founder Bill Gates donated $100,000.

Businesses across Washington supported same-sex marriage because they believed it was critical to retaining the state's skilled workforce. Many business leaders denounced Republican myths that same-sex marriage would "kill jobs" because it required businesses to spend more money on employee benefits. Throughout the Referendum 74 campaign conservatives had fewer reasons to justify why gays and lesbians should have fewer rights. Unlike the 2008 election, six states had already boarded the gay marriage bandwagon. The legislative and judiciary victories in those states were crucial for advocates to illustrate that same-sex marriage is not an extreme idea.

Throughout the campaign I collected more and more minute data to scan the political terrain. I frequently checked Nate Silver's

FiveThirtyEight blog because it had useful information pertaining to political analysis. The results of Referendum 74 truly depended on turnout. If Washington enjoyed a robust voter turnout (which exceeded 70%) it was likely that advocates of gay marriage would celebrate their first victory.

Although Washington is situated on the "Left Coast," this state has a relatively conservative history. Since 1965 Republicans have controlled the Secretary of State's office. During the 1994 Republican Revolution, Republicans picked up six congressional seats—the most of any state during that year. In addition, Governor Christine Gregoire was first elected by a margin of only 133 votes. To put that in perspective, Washington's 2004 gubernatorial race was closer than the 2000 Presidential Election in Florida. It took three recounts and several lawsuits before Governor Gregoire was sworn into office. Despite the fact Democrats controlled the legislature, Republicans secured enough votes to pass their version of a state budget.

Washington's political geography is extremely interesting. Despite the fact that roughly two-thirds of the state's land area is located east of the Cascade Mountains—most of the state's population resides in the Seattle Metropolitan Area (which only consists of three of the state's thirty-nine counties). Whenever a Republican wins a statewide election, they must perform well in Western Washington. In 1984 Ronald Reagan won the state of Washington by a comfortable margin. His victory was attributed to the fact voters in King, Snohomish, and Pierce County supported him. If a Republican is unable to outright win King County, they must reduce their opponent's margin of victory.

During the late 1980s, Washington's demographics gradually shifted from red to light blue. As many western states continue to urbanize, states that were once reliably red were slowly becoming less and less conservative. A major reason behind Washington's political shift is that more people are living in fewer, but more populous counties. As a result, King County is home to nearly one-third of the state's electorate. In 1972 there were only 212,509 Democrats residing in King County, by 2012 the number of Democrats increased to 668,004. In just forty years—the number of Democratic voters tripled in the state's largest county alone. It was crucial for proponents of Referendum 74 to rack up substantial margins in King County because it could easily determine the fate of same-sex marriage.

The final days before the 2012 Presidential Election were extremely nerve-wracking. Once again, I was an emotional wreck not because of Obama's re-election, but whether proponents of same-sex marriage were going to win at the ballot box. By May 2012 thirty state constitutions outlawed same-sex marriage and not once did proponents of same-sex marriage secure a single victory. I couldn't stop but think about the feeling I faced when I was seventeen years old and how it felt to have my future appear on the ballot. My fate lied in the hands of nearly 4 million registered voters.

Shortly before Election Day, I pulled Claire aside and expressed my doubts about the success of Referendum 74. I told her that no state has ever approved same-sex marriage via public vote. During my conversation with Claire, she asked me if I ever thought same-sex marriage was possible in Washington, I swiftly nodded, *"yes."* Throughout the election cycle Claire was extremely supportive of my desire to help others. I was extremely thankful that she was with me during this remarkable journey.

November 6, 2012 marked the day proponents of same-sex marriage faced their most serious test. Gay marriage advocates were fighting to make history. Six months after voters in North Carolina outlawed same-sex marriage, Washington finally had its turn to provide input on this national discussion. During this time several federal court cases regarding the constitutionality of the Defense of Marriage Act (DOMA) were awaiting the United States Supreme Court. Lawyers in New York and Massachusetts convinced federal judges to invalidate Section 3 of the Defense of Marriage Act because it prevented the federal government from recognizing marriages between same-sex couples in six states. When same-sex marriage was first legal in Connecticut, same-sex couples were not entitled to any of the 1,138 federal benefits enjoyed by opposite-sex couples. As a result, several state attorney generals urged the United States Supreme Court to allow the federal government to recognize same-sex marriage at the state level.

There was no question in my mind that the outcome of same-sex marriage ballot measures in Maine, Maryland, and Washington would not only influence *if* the United States Supreme Court agreed to hear a DOMA case, but *how* the court would side on this matter.

On Election Day I skipped my landscape architecture class (which met in the late afternoon). Well before, I decided that I would not attend any afternoon classes because I could not focus in lecture while my rights were in flux. Just before 4:30 pm I ran to my house and turned on the television to watch the election results. Throughout the evening I was on edge. I turned on MSNBC and sent frequent text messages to Claire asking her if she had any information regarding the latest election results. All my roommates centered around the living room as if it were a Super Bowl party.

Unlike Washington, Maine and Maryland do not vote-by-mail. As a result, those states are more expedient when it comes to tabulating election results. Just before MSNBC called Ohio to President Obama voters in Maine and Maryland both approved same-sex marriage. When I discovered this news—I *screamed* with joy because the glass ceiling was finally shattered.

From that moment on, the mood of election night changed from uncertainty to optimism. People on my street launched fireworks and elation filled the streets of Capitol Hill. Watching advocates of gay marriage propel three ballot victories in one night reaffirmed the fact they were no longer a silent minority. The gay rights movement refused to be defined by thirty states that voted against their interests. November 6, 2012 marked the beginning of a new chapter because conservatives could no longer say gays and lesbians can never win.

Shortly after 10:00 pm the Secretary of State began posting election results on the agency's website. I was constantly refreshing my Internet browser because I wanted to retrieve the most recent election data. Once returns were initially posted, Referendum 74 was only leading in eight of Washington's thirty-nine counties. On election night Referendum 74 was leading by a margin of 51.78%. Since Washington is a vote-by-mail state, final election results are not known for several days. In fact, most media outlets refused to call that race.

Three days after the election, Preserve Marriage Washington finally conceded and supporters of same-sex marriage officially declared victory. Referendum 74 had grown its lead to 53.7% and was ahead in ten counties. Referendum 74 performed strongly in King County (which is home to over 30% of Washington's population). According to the *Seattle Times*, Referendum 74 passed in Seattle by 82%. Twenty cities in King County voted in favor of same-sex marriage by a margin greater than 60%. Support was also strong in cities like Bellevue, Redmond, and Sammamish. Another important factor to solidifying the success of Referendum 74 was voter turnout. According to the Secretary of State's office, voter turnout reached 81.25%.

When Referendum 74 passed I felt like a new person. The last time my spirit felt so invigorated was shortly after the 2008 election. I was glad that I transferred to the University of Washington because it gave me the opportunity to continue fighting for equal rights. Had I stayed at UConn, I would not have the opportunity to share my story with people 3,000 miles away. Living on the other side of the country taught me there are far more issues that unite mankind. As I traveled across America and campaigned for human rights, it allowed me to connect with others on a personal level. These past nine months reinforced my initial idea that social acceptance is a universal desire which spans across all walks of life. People around the world regardless of their race, social status, religion, gender, disability, sexual orientation, or age want to feel a degree of social acceptance.

The results of Referendum 74 reaffirm the arguments I reiterated when I testified in favor of North Carolina's School Violence Prevention Act. In 2009 I expressed that, "Everyone has been discriminated, discrimination hurts, discrimination is wrong." The voters of Washington reaffirm my vision that people want to belong to inclusive communities and form harmonious friendships. Throughout the campaign I stressed that Referendum 74 was not only about marriage—its purpose was telling others they are not an "ugly duckling" for loving another person. The faces of Referendum 74 included young students like me who struggled to come to terms with their sexual orientation. Referendum 74 extended the same hope I was fortunate to receive once the Connecticut Supreme Court upheld the rights of gays and lesbians.

A couple of days after the election Claire approached me and told me in front of a group of students, *"You can finally get married!"* For once I was willing to poke fun at myself because the election was over. As I bubbled with enthusiasm my face turned bright pink. Seconds later, I *pounded* my chest and bellowed, *"Yes...I could marry my college crush for once!"*

That afternoon was full of laughter. I was finally able to close another political chapter. I frequently reference this story whenever I introduce myself to new friends. Shortly before I left Gould Hall, I walked up to Claire and pulled her aside. I quietly told her, *"miracles happen and dreams do come true just like they did in Connecticut!"* I gave Claire a tight hug because I wanted to thank her for her support over the past several months. I was also amazed to see her become politically active just like I was during high school.

Same-sex marriage was officially legalized on December 6, 2012. County offices in King and Thurston opened at midnight after the measure was certified, with celebrations in support outside of several government offices. After nine long months, the fight for same-sex marriage had finally ended.

9 FIGHTING FOR ASSISTED SUICIDE

"You gain strength, courage and confidence by every experience in which you really stop to look fear in the face. You are able to say to yourself, 'I have lived through this horror. I can take the next thing that comes along.' You must do the thing you think you cannot do."
-Eleanor Roosevelt

My college crush had a mix of Dutch and Polish ancestry. His appearance resembled Mark Rutte, the Prime Minister of the Netherlands. When I first met this handsome stranger (during my sophomore year), I asked myself, *"What's his ancestry?"* I wanted to discover his ethnic heritage so I could find men that shared his physical appearance.

On May 20, 2012 I spent several hours (well past my bedtime) researching The Netherlands. When I researched the country's political history I came across the issue of assisted suicide.

Assisted Suicide occurs when a doctor prescribes lethal drugs to an individual living with a terminal illness who knowingly has less than six months to live. This legislation encompasses several safeguards. For instance, a terminally ill patient needs to send a written request and oral request to their doctor explaining *why* they want a lethal dose of medication. Any patient can rescind this request at anytime. In addition, two witnesses must accompany the patient whenever they make their request for any lethal medication. One of those witnesses *can't* be related to the patient *or* be listed as a beneficiary of the patient's estate. States with assisted suicide legislation require patients to be mentally competent before any prescriptions are given. Doctors are also required to verify medical records and confirm the patient's diagnosis before any medication is dispensed.

When I first became aware of this issue only three states permitted assisted suicide. Washington and Oregon passed assisted suicide ballot measures in 2008 and 1994. Montana first permitted assisted suicide in 2009 following a landmark decision from the state supreme court (in *Baxter v. Montana*).

What I found most alarming was learning how poorly assisted suicide legislation was being implemented in Montana. In 2008 a group of four physicians sued the State of Montana for not allowing their patient Robert Baxter to have the option of taking lethal medication to end his pain.

Robert was a seventy-six-year-old truck driver from Billings. He was diagnosed with an advanced stage of lymphocytic leukemia. The plaintiffs representing Baxter argued that the Montana Constitution protects a person's right to privacy and self-determination.

On December 5, 2008 a lower district court in Montana ruled in favor of Baxter, stating that the, "constitutional rights of individual privacy and human dignity, taken together, encompass the right of a competent terminally ill patient to die with dignity." Baxter lost his battle to leukemia that same day.

The Montana Attorney General appealed this case to the Montana Supreme Court and oral arguments were heard on September 2, 2009. On December 31, 2009 the Montana Supreme Court ruled in favor of Baxter. It stated that, while the state's Constitution did not guarantee a right to physician-assisted suicide, there was: "nothing in Montana Supreme Court precedent or Montana statutes indicating that physician aid in dying is against public policy."

Although a high court in Montana determined that assisted suicide is not unconstitutional, this ruling was never fully implemented because there are no legal safeguards for doctors to safely carry this practice. Last year, SB 116 was introduced. This provision not only reverses the *Baxter v. Montana* decision, but it criminalizes any doctor who performs assisted suicide with up to 10 years in prison and a $50,000 fine.

Reconnected

On May 21, 2012 I awoke to a world knowing it housed people who had no respect for mankind. Montana lawmakers blocked assisted suicide legislation and there was nothing I could do. I felt powerless because people on Earth were not doing enough to ensure others experienced a peaceful transition to heaven. I was alarmed that people on Earth wanted to lengthen the suffering of a malignant illness. The Montana legislature's failure to provide *adequate* relief caused Robert Baxter's health to severely deteriorate. During his final months, Robert lost so much weight he couldn't sit because his skin hurt. Each morning Robert awoke to a world where he experienced more and more pain. He lived a life where he could not control his own destiny. Furthermore, Robert was forced to witness his own health deteriorate.

As I encountered this disturbing truth, my first class was scheduled in less than two hours. Although I felt empty, I did my best to put on a brave face because my calendar was booked with numerous events. Monday morning was extremely difficult because I recognized that I lived in a world where only six jurisdictions allow terminally ill patients to determine their own death.

As I walked to Gould Hall I tried to disregard what occurred last night. I convinced myself, "Robert Baxter's death has no greater meaning to what I experienced." Once I entered class I was unusually quiet. I showed no emotion. Whenever a fellow student told a joke or revealed a funny story I remained terse. My depression was so severe; it didn't matter what anyone said or did to help me.

I couldn't pay attention because I wanted to understand *why* someone supported the idea of watching someone live through his or her *worst* stages. As my instructor was speaking, the song "Born Slippery" by Underworld played inside my head. The first minute of this song is really somber. Feelings of sadness and grief resonate immediately. As this song played inside my head, I thought about the human life cycle. Everyone originates in the same condition and leaves in a much different state of mind. The world is plagued with tremendous man-made inequities. The lengthy decay of a person's body is extremely unimaginable. Humans have created legal barriers, which prolong a person's worst pain during their final months. This type of cruelty illustrates how some policies do not receive enough thought.

I experienced a gruesome flashback during class. I left thinking I would be gone for five minutes. As soon as I entered the bathroom, I locked myself inside a stall and sat on the floor. Before I was able to pull any toilet paper my face was covered in tears. For the next seven minutes I cried hysterically. At first I was not able to comprehend exactly what I was crying about. Although I was deeply upset, I struggled to pinpoint what exactly fueled my emotions. Since I was unable to determine the cause of my grief I tried walking back to class. Once I left the bathroom another *violent outburst* occurred. My tears were pouring onto the cement ground of Gould Hall because I hadn't finished coping with my grandfather's death.

After not seeing my grandfather in over five years I came across a seventy-six-year-old truck driver who mirrored Charles Filer. As I learned more about Robert Baxter, I realized these men shared countless similarities. Robert and Charles were both adored by their families, enjoyed outdoor activities, and deserved to experience a peaceful death. Although Charles never met Robert Baxter, I could not help but think I was staring at my grandfather.

Robert's blue eyes replicated the person who never forgot to send me a birthday card. Looking at his face unleashed five years of insecurity, pain, and guilt. As soon as I was able to grasp the depth and complexity of this issue, I looked through a small window beneath a private staircase and muttered; "I'm *really* sorry...I'm *really* sorry. I feel *really* bad right now." Each time I reiterated the word *"really"* I experienced more and more guilt because the memories of April 26, 2007 resurfaced. As tears poured down my face, I felt selfish for not spending more time with Charles. In addition, I was infuriated that lawmakers in Montana didn't care how painful or prolonged my grandfather's death was. It sickened me that Republicans enjoyed watching innocent people suffer. Once I was able to identify why I was in such agony, I wanted to speak with someone so I could heal.

While I was meandering through Gould Hall I saw a classmate exit the bathroom. I never spent much time talking to this individual, but I was willing to share my story if he was the only person around. I walked up to Adam Fahlstrom and called out his name. I asked in a shockingly calm manner, *"Could I speak with you by any chance? I really have something important to tell you."* Once he agreed, I directed him to the corner of a concrete staircase. Shortly after entering this secluded area, I struggled to compose myself.

I calmly said to Adam; *"I'm really sorry* if it takes me longer to gather my thoughts...these past several hours have been *extremely* painful."* I first opened up about the time I was sixteen years old. I expressed how being the youngest in my family is a real disadvantage because my older cousins and siblings were able to invite my grandfather to graduation parties, weddings, and baby showers. I told Adam about Charles and how he spent much of his life in Northwest Ohio. I also revealed he was a World War II veteran.

People who experience introverted sensing have a remarkable ability to recall past events as if they are currently reliving it. Despite being twenty-one years old, I found myself slipping back into my "sixteen-year-old self." When I say the term, "sixteen-year-old self" I'm referring to a previous mindset. During this conversation I unconsciously entered another reality. I started this intense discussion by informing Adam:

> "When someone I love in my life experiences a major decline in their health, I'm more likely to withdraw from that person. It's *really* painful for me to watch someone decline and know they are leaving. To help myself cope, I have silently detached myself so it's not as painful once they die.
>
> One afternoon my grandfather was doing work on his roof. He fell off a ladder and almost died. Since that horrific accident, his health was never the same. He would come in and out of the hospital on a regular basis. It was *agonizing* watching his quality-of-life decline each day. The worst part was that I couldn't even *recognize* him when I last saw him in the hospital."

When I reiterated the words, "I couldn't even *recognize* him" I was overwhelmed with sadness. It was so graphic. I felt a sense of mortification and humility because I was guilty of the same loathsome actions as my paraprofessional. For nearly seven years I vilified her for leaving my life. As I spoke to Adam through a previous mindset I realized that I was just as inferior. During my grandfather's final months, I also silently withdrew and didn't provide any formal notice. The same hatred I held against Cheryl for seven years was the way I viewed myself internally.

As our conversation progressed, things shifted to Montana. I told Adam in 2009 the Montana Supreme Court ruled that assisted suicide was not unconstitutional under Montana law. I also discussed that many doctors are fearful of performing this procedure because the legislature has refused to pass any legal safeguards that would implement this ruling. As I recounted this painful story my emotions destabilized. I told Adam in such a heavy voice:

> "*It kills me* that members of the Montana legislature are making the final days of countless people so painful! *It kills me* that people don't have the right to peacefully transition to heaven! I don't care what *your* political affiliation is, *no one* should be forced to *suffer...*"

Even though my grandfather's body was buried five years ago; the aftermath of his death was happening live. This moment was very surreal because images of his declining health appeared slightly skewed by Robert Baxter's illness. Despite attempts to leave behind personal grief, I realized there is no such truth as "being over" or "no longer happening" because the mind uses memory to retain painful moments throughout life. Memory causes humans to re-experience gruesome and unimaginable flashbacks. Sometimes such horrific occurrences exist timelessly. Although I was a grown adult, I couldn't control my *violent* emotional outbursts.

As tears *poured* down my shirt I felt more and more anguish. Towards the end of our conversation I couldn't provide any eye contact. I couldn't love or embrace anyone on the same plane because I was so meager. As Adam reached to give me a hug I automatically *sunk* into his lap. I wrapped my arms around his entire waist and squeezed. Even though I was twenty-one years old—I was still a child. I couldn't remember the last time I experienced such intense emotional contact. As Adam held me I was assured *immediate forgiveness*. His warmth rivals how most parents embrace their first child. Despite past mistakes, Adam was there to pour his love. I was gratified by his presence and compassion because it was truly a reflection of God's miracles.

For the first time I felt so proud to be a Washingtonian. As I clinched my arms around Adam's waist he informed me about the moment he voted in favor of assisted suicide. During the past year I was fixated on present issues. As a result, I was cynical at the fact it took Washington state four years to follow Connecticut and pass same-sex marriage. I was not only frustrated that things didn't follow my timeline, but I was equally annoyed that my basic needs were being ignored.

May 21, 2012 changed my entire outlook on life because I didn't need a notarized certificate to feel loved. Every act of warmth and kindness is a reflection of God's work. Every dimension of time is equally important. The past, present, and future not only form a profound continuum, but too many individuals don't recognize that miracles and dreams occur across each dimension of time.

Before Adam left I recognized Washington was already on the right side of history. Even though I couldn't receive a marriage license that afternoon I felt a sense of peace. Everything I told myself earlier about states with anti-gay laws was totally self-constructed. At that moment, I decided to start campaigning for Death with Dignity Acts across the United States because I learned that change is possible.

Political Fight in Montana

My first experience advocating for assisted suicide occurred in Montana. Roughly a month after I had my conversation with Adam I contacted State Senator Anders Blewett. Senator Blewett represents Great Falls; he repeatedly introduced legislation to codify the *Baxter v. Montana* ruling into statue. In my letter, I thanked him for advocating SB 167 by saying:

> "I want to add my voice to the list of supporters who want the Montana legislature to codify the *Baxter v. Montana* ruling into law. It's important that doctors are granted the needed legal protections so they can legally perform assisted suicide. I want you to know that you have supporters outside of Montana who are cheering for you."

As I was working to build a coalition in Montana for assisted suicide I knew that I had to take my fight to the Attorney General. Steve Bullock was the Attorney General of Montana—his office appealed the lower court decision upholding assisted suicide. I knew if the legislature wouldn't act, I would have to convince the Attorney General to issue a formal legal opinion.

In 2012 Steve Bullock was in the middle of a tough gubernatorial campaign. Regardless of the election cycle, I decided to contact his office because I wanted my voice to be heard. In my letter I explained that *Baxter v. Montana* was such a narrow ruling. In addition, I stressed, "under the current law, there's nothing to protect a doctor from prosecution. I'm writing to your office because I hope you can issue a legal opinion to codify *Baxter v. Montana* into law."

Connecticut Death with Dignity Act

On December 27, 2012 I started campaigning for assisted suicide in Connecticut. Last month voters in Massachusetts narrowly rejected Question 2. Although assisted suicide was not approved this time around, I was not going to fade away anytime soon. My fight for a person's right to self-determination was just beginning. During the final days of December, I reached out to Connecticut State Representative Matt Lesser. Earlier in the year I worked with Representative Lesser to help advance early voting in Connecticut. In my letter to Representative Lesser I expressed:

> "My name is Gabriel and I am a 22-year-old college student. As the legislative session begins, I really hope you could introduce an assisted suicide bill. Oregon and Washington have legalized physician-assisted suicide through voter initiative. The Death with Dignity Act in both states provides protections to doctors who are willing to write prescriptions to help end the life of a terminally ill patient.
>
> My grandfather became extremely ill at the age of 90 and it was really painful to watch the health of someone I knew deteriorate. It was extremely agonizing not knowing when my grandfather was going to leave. A week before his death I visited him in the hospital and I did not even *recognize* him.
>
> I want to add my voice to the list of supporters who want Connecticut to adopt a Death with Dignity Act

because I support the right to self-determination. It is important that doctors are granted the needed legal protections so they can legally perform assisted suicide.

I want to thank you for considering this proposal because I know this issue is really sensitive. Even if this proposal does not pass, it would be wonderful if you could help begin a conversation on this important issue."

An hour after I wrote this message, Representative Lesser's name appeared inside my inbox. As soon as I opened his message I was surprised with two great sentences. He first thanked me for sharing my story and promised to introduce legislation next month. Before the end of the afternoon, Representative Lesser encouraged me to testify in favor of this issue. He also mentioned that convincing arguments from impassioned citizens were key to winning over the hearts and minds of state lawmakers.

On the following morning the Connecticut Death with Dignity Act received another major boost. The *Hartford Courant* editorial board released its annual to-do list for the upcoming legislative session. A major issue the editorial board believed needed to be addressed was enacting the Connecticut Death with Dignity Act. The *Hartford Courant* cited the importance of passing assisted suicide and why people should have a right to determine their own death. The editorial board explicitly revealed; "After 15 years, Oregon's law has not been abused—only about 600 people have taken the lethal medication under physician supervision—and the statute has been upheld by the U.S. Supreme Court." As soon as I finished reading this article I grabbed a pair of scissors and secretly tucked this article inside my bag. The ingredients to advancing assisted suicide were already in the cards. I was excited that the state's largest newspaper pressured lawmakers to take action.

On January 9, 2013 State Senator Ed Meyer introduced SB 48. This bill was referred to the Senate Judiciary Committee. Nine days later I wrote to Senator Meyer because I hoped to offer my support. Later that afternoon, I heard another call to go forth and help others. Eric Emanuelson, the Legislative Aide for Senator Meyer reached out to me. In a brief message Eric (introduced himself and) encouraged me to send any useful testimony.

I could not help but feel I was reliving January 23, 2009. During the next several hours I sat alone aside my desk. My objective was to detail what happened. Two dates surfaced as I was writing. April 21, 2007 was the last time I saw my grandfather and May 21, 2012 marked the day I relived his death. Those two gruesome days never escaped my memory. The most painful aspect of writing such a graphic story is explaining someone's death in great detail. It's incredibly heartbreaking to share the moment someone lost his or her independence. It's *unimaginably* agonizing having to write about the final hours of somebody's life. What's even worse—not knowing the final thoughts of someone you love.

In less than eight hours I finished writing. After composing compelling testimony, I quickly reviewed my work before sending it to Eric. I did my best to inform members of the Connecticut Assembly key provisions of SB 48, and how terminally ill patients will gain a peace of mind knowing their end-of-life choices will be respected. I notified Eric that although I couldn't visit Hartford to testify in person, I hope Senator Meyer will read my story in front of the Senate Judiciary Committee.

Once I overcame this personal fear, I contacted my friend Adam Fahlstrom. I informed him that legislation to permit assisted suicide was recently introduced in Connecticut. In addition, I shared with him the fact I prepared written arguments for SB 48. I finished my message by telling him I argued in front of two state legislatures in less than four years.

My determination to helping others showed no signs of receding. Even though SB 48 did not pass during the legislative session, I accomplished my top goal—starting an important conversation in state government. In the end, I prepared gruesome testimony because there is no such thing as being *too compassionate*. Whenever I fight to break social constructs or change public policy, the parties at greater fault are those who are too dispassionate.

Although the journey to enact the Death with Dignity Act is far from over, I fought to my greatest capacity to champion legislation which improved a person's right to determine their own death. I pursued this crucial cause because I believe the cost of inaction is far worse than the cost of making a mistake. Another year politicians ignore this issue is another year patients suffer. I intend to rigorously fight against any legal barriers, which prevent individuals from enjoying a peaceful transition to heaven.

10 TAKING ACTION

"Our values call upon us to care about the lives of people we will never meet."
-Barrack Obama

After fighting for same-sex marriage on both coasts I spent some time advancing this issue abroad. I first became fascinated in geopolitics when I took a class taught by Tish Lopez called GEOG 431: Gender and Geography. Her class not only stimulated my interest in human rights, but it inspired me to research the living conditions of the LGBT community around the world. During her class, I was deeply disappointed to learn the rights of gays and lesbians faced a major setback during the Arab Spring. What I found most disappointing was watching voters in Egypt elect an extremist government. Although I was initially hopeful that political revolutions across the Middle East would pave the way for gays and lesbians to enjoy greater dignity, I was wrong. As a result, I decided to take action because my duty was to do everything in my power to advocate for human rights.

President Obama Contacts Me

Before taking action I researched best practices regarding human rights policy (as it pertains to the LGBT community). When I examine the political landscape of gay rights around the world, three factors stood out: advanced economies, social welfare, and geography. According to the *International Monetary Fund*, thirty-six countries are classified as "advanced economies." 22 (of these 36) countries recognize same-sex unions at the national level. In addition, each country with the exception of Singapore decriminalized sexual acts between same-sex couples.

The *Human Development Index* measures social welfare using a unique formula, which incorporates life expectancy, mean years of schooling, and gross national income. The objective of the *Human Development Index* is to benchmark how countries across the world perform when it comes to providing education, healthcare, and economic opportunities to its citizens. According to the *2013 Human Development Index* report, nine of the top ten performing countries (with the exception of Japan) extend legal protections to same-sex couples.

Generally speaking, gay rights enjoys, "more support" across Canada, United States, Australia, New Zealand, and Western Europe. I use the term "more support" because no country has achieved a perfect human rights record. Although my findings suggest the geography of gay rights is more prevalent in nations with higher socio-economic rankings, there are exceptions. For example, South Africa (a country where nearly a quarter of the population lives under $1.25 a day) became the first country in the southern hemisphere to permit same-sex marriage. Although South Africa's legal system ensures equality for the LGBT community, gays and lesbians are subject to inhumane policies across the globe.

Same-sex couples are subject to criminal penalties in seventy-eight countries. A majority of the world's sodomy laws are concentrated throughout the Middle East, Africa, and isolated pockets of Asia. The most loathsome element of sodomy laws is that it not only prohibits gay men from having sex, but it allows countries to create a double standard. Although Malaysia and Jamaica permit lesbians to legally engage in sex: gay men are subject to whip lashings by Malaysian authorities, face life imprisonment in Barbados, and must perform a decade of hard labor in Jamaica.

Although I do not like to stereotype developing nations as being *less* tolerant—the data in front of me reveals many developed countries have led the fight towards advancing the interests of the LGBT community. In 2011, British Prime Minister David Cameron proposed a law that would drastically reduce foreign aid to countries that impose sodomy laws. Shortly after discovering his proposal, I urged President Barrack Obama to withhold foreign aid from countries with sodomy laws because I want to hold leaders within the African Union and Arab League accountable. I also plan to send a message to the international community that I was fighting for human rights:

> "British Prime Minister David Cameron sent a clear message to countries which violate human rights. He stated any country that does not decriminalize homosexual acts *will* have their foreign aid *eliminated* or *drastically* reduced. I strongly support Cameron's proposal because gay rights are human rights. I believe the United States should not be funneling money to governments that have no respect for humanity. People should be able to live freely and each country should uphold human dignity. It is sad that several countries have refused to sign the United Nation's pledge calling for the decriminalization of homosexuality worldwide.
>
> I hope the United States will join the United Kingdom (and other European allies) to promote human dignity throughout the world. I personally believe many countries need to understand that punishing people for loving someone (of the same gender) is *wrong.*
>
> Sodomy laws are *cruel* and *inhumane* because they have empowered governments and religious institutions to take advantage of innocent people. Unless the United States withholds foreign aid and demands the repeal of sodomy laws throughout Africa and Middle East, countless crimes against humanity will continue to occur. I am encouraging the United States to hold countries accountable because people should not be criminalized based on their sexual orientation or gender identity. I hope someday in my lifetime homosexuals will be able to enjoy the same rights that people in other countries enjoy which is respect, tolerance, and the opportunity to live in peace."

Once I wrote to the White House I believed my message would get lost. I even asked myself, "*Why* would the President of the United States ever take the time to listen to a twenty-one-year-old gay rights activist?" For over a month I never got a response. One afternoon I received a letter from President Obama. Once I opened his message I realized someone was listening. On December 6, 2011 President Obama issued a Presidential Memorandum directing federal agencies to consider gay rights when allocating foreign aid to each country. This provision not only combats the criminalization of gays and lesbians by foreign governments, but it enhances efforts to ensure the United States engages with countries in order to advance the human rights of LGBT individuals. In addition, President Obama expressed his support for gay rights:

> "We *must* stand united to protect liberty and justice for all our citizens, and I appreciate your perspective on lesbian, gay, bisexual, and transgender (LGBT) rights. My Administration has taken a number of steps to address issues affecting the LGBT community. While we have made great strides, *much work remains* in the quest for equality for LGBT individuals."

Once I finished reading my letter from President Obama I realized I must continue fighting for others. During my final year of college I researched nations with "strong records" of gay rights. One country that caught my attention was South Africa. No story is more remarkable when it comes to the progress of human rights than watching Nelson Mandela sign the Constitution of South Africa into law. In 1996, South Africa became the first country to include sexual orientation as a protected-class in a federal constitution. Although I deeply admired Nelson Mandela for advancing the rights of gays and lesbians, I never imagined my message would someday reach him before I finished college.

Thanking Nelson Mandela

On June 12, 2013 my family was arriving at SeaTac International Airport to attend my Graduation. In just three days I was scheduled to return my keys to my landlord. For just a brief moment I looked outside my small window (which points towards the Olympic Mountains). I asked myself, "What could I do to make my final days in Seattle more fulfilling?" At this moment, a light bulb went off inside my head. I decided that I was going to reach out to former South African President Nelson Mandela and thank him for making human dignity a constitutional right and for championing South Africa to being the world's first country to protect gays and lesbians from discrimination in their constitution.

Just before I left my house to meet my family at the airport, I went online to research the Nelson Mandela Foundation. Since 2004 Nelson Mandela retired from public life. As a result, it became more and more difficult to contact him. At the age of 94, the former President was staying in and out of hospitals. Over the past several months his health was slowly deteriorating. I was ominous that President Mandela would not live much longer. As a result, I wrote a letter to his office before he died. In my letter I wrote:

> "My name is Gabriel Filer and I study human rights and public policy in the United States. You have inspired me to fight for better laws. I am *awed* at your political accomplishments. I want to thank you for fighting to pass the Constitution of South Africa.
>
> The Constitution of South Africa is a model for human rights because it acknowledges a person's right to human dignity and self-determination. This document demonstrates that you can find opportunity inside human tragedy. I really want to thank you for making sure that South Africa included sexual orientation as a protected-class. Your hard work continues to open doors to so many people around the world. The progressive Constitution you signed in 1996 has extended numerous rights and responsibilities to the LGBT community.
>
> Your passion for community advocacy and public policy is deeply inspiring. You have empowered countless people around the world to ask for better laws. Your thoughts are with me. You have a lot to be proud of."

Once I sent my letter, I did not expect to receive a response. Whenever I contacted someone who served in public office, I rarely hear back.

Two days before my graduation I was awakened to an astonishing surprise. On June 13, 2013 someone from the Nelson

Mandela Foundation responded. Ethel Arends is the Records Management Coordinator. She thanked me for writing to President Mandela and assured me that my message would be conveyed with the former South African President. At that moment, I was gratified to know my voice was never lost.

Once I received this message I contacted Sabrina Ryan. I told my roommate that during my final days of college someone from the Nelson Mandela Foundation reached out to me. I explained how amazed I was to hear from one of the world's most influential leaders.

Sabrina said something which stuck with me, "We get so caught up in our daily lives it's easy to forget the treasures that human beings are capable of through compassion and understanding." Sabrina recognized the importance of living each day to the fullest. She understood that people should remove themself from reality because great ideas emerge when people are introspective and set meaningful goals.

First Love

Sabrina Ryan was well aware of my deep fascination about international law and human rights. Over the past several months my friendship with her grew tremendously. A defining moment during our friendship occurred on one unforgettable night. Shortly after my other roommates left the house, I grabbed my laptop and showed her a picture of my college crush. The first words I expressed once I opened my screen were; *"Isn't this man the hottest person alive...What ethnicity do you think he is?"*

As soon as I closed my computer Sabrina's jaw dropped. She was shocked that I introduced this attractive man. I caught Sabrina by complete surprise because she witnessed a mysterious aspect of my inner life emerge. I told her about the time I met a silent handsome stranger and how this experience taught me the importance of finding wholeness each day I lived. I expressed how crucial "last words" are in human relationships because they determine the attitudes and aura of both parties whenever they are reunited.

The story I shared with Sabrina began on January 22, 2011. It started off like any normal day because I stepped outside into another afternoon of everlasting rain shadow. Winters in Western

Washington experience (mild temperatures and) frequent overcast because the moisture from the Olympic Mountains block excessive rain from entering Puget Sound. Although Seattle is immune from most extreme weather events, it receives constant rain shadow because most low-lying clouds are trapped between the Cascade and Olympic Mountains.

I spent much of this day working extensively on projects for GEOG 277: Geography of Cities. As I was tediously programing Census data into an Excel spreadsheet I decided to schedule a late lunch break. I grabbed the purple and gold sweatshirt I wore each day and ran to a nearby dining hall. This was another routine—I planned to purchase the same item at the same store, and return home where I finish my homework.

As I was completing another weekend routine I was slapped by the presence of a tall dark-haired slender man wearing a black hoodie. His crystal blue eyes immediately caught my attention. I physically examined this handsome stranger (like most men examine women) from head to toe. I did not stare for *too long* because I was not ready to draw any attention to myself. Once I finished inspecting his body for five seconds, I quietly muttered, *"What's his ethnic composition...where could I find men that are just as attractive as him?"*

This man stood out—I never saw anyone who looked like him. His crystal blue eyes, thick eyebrows, and setback eye sockets boldly distinguished his facial characteristics from most people I ever met. His dark brown hair was roughly combed straight. Although his hair length was short, it was tastefully messy. His pale skin beautifully contrasted against his dark hair and light blue eyes. His skin was so light—his entire face would turn pink during a polar vortex. His blue eyes, fair skin, and (straight) hair texture suggest this irresistible nerd was Scandinavian, however the shape of his nose and dark hair color implied he was from Eastern Europe. Once I merged these two ideas I thought he was Finnish (an ethnic group practically nonexistent in Connecticut).

For the next several months, I tried to crack his ethnic code, however, I had to approach this student in order to determine his true background. When I was in college I worked as a cashier at a dining hall. The best part of this job was seeing this handsome stranger walk by. Whenever he came to order food I supplied him with *generous* portions. I didn't hesitate to give him special treatment. At first I was too shy to even say anything. His tranquil and reserved exterior magnified my intimidation to even ask his name or major. It took several weeks for me to acquire the confidence to simply say, *"How is your day?"*

Chris was the perfect eye candy. At times, his body appeared to be painted. This twenty-two-year-old tucked in his shirt to increase the visibility of certain areas. Around Valentine's Day I was in for a real treat because Chris dropped some change. As I was finishing a customer's order my full attention shifted to him. While Chris was bending down I saw his curvaceous features come to life. Even though Chris didn't rival Kim Kardashian, his ass was very impressive. The excitement I felt examining his ass is similar to how most men gape at female breasts. Although Chris could easily be judged as just a skinny white guy, I view him as somebody with an extremely lustful body. I wasn't necessarily aroused at the size of his body parts, what stimulated me the most was watching him use effeminate techniques to provoke sexual tease. One thing Chris demonstrated is that men are just as sexualized as women.

One late April afternoon I faced this heartthrob at the cash register. I asked him how his day was. He told me, "Things are going *great!*" Before I knew it, he quickly asked me how I was. I responded in a very nonchalant manner, "I'm alright."

After hearing nothing but silence from Chris, he warmly smiled and said, "I wish you were feeling better than *just alright!*" Once I heard him state those remarks my entire face turned pink. As Chris walked away his jeans stole my attention once again. This time he lowered his pants to reveal his boxers—which resembled a navy Scottish plaid. These undergarments contained a complex series of white and pink stripes. Once I peaked at his pink stripes I immediately felt aroused. The fact my deepest crush wore pink undies solidified my desire to pursue a relationship with him. I thought to myself, "I can't wait to see this man try women's underwear and take off his clothes! *Married life will be such a blast!*"

By May I became more and more comfortable casually approaching this individual. I started off by asking his name and major. He told me his name was "Chris" and majored in "Psychology." Throughout the quarter I did my best to use humor. On one occasion I voiced how I felt like *"Charlie Sheen on steroids!"* I did my best to make this customer laugh because I really liked him. I didn't want to portray myself as too outrageous, however I wanted to distinguish myself from other people. At the end of the day, I didn't want this person to forget me.

Shortly before the school year came to a close, I asked Chris where he was from and what his summer plans were. This was the first time I tried to discover his background. He mentioned that he has two hometowns: Vancouver, WA and Oceanside, CA.

Although he was raised in Southwest Washington, his family recently moved to Southern California for family reasons. Once he shared his personal background he asked me what I was up to. I told him that I was spending the summer in Connecticut. Once I told him that I was from Connecticut his face was covered in *shock*. He was really surprised to learn that I grew up on the other side of the country.

The casual conversations I experienced with this customer became instrumental when it came to establishing a personal connection. By the time I left for summer break Chris was no longer a stranger. Although I did not acquire a lot of personal information from him, this experience taught me the importance of approaching others. I pursued my relationship with Chris using baby steps. A major regret I hold to this day was that I took this individual's presence for granted. Even though I really loved this person, I allowed my fear of social rejection to overcome any desire to step outside my comfort zone. Someday I planned to ask him on a date. I really wanted to take my relationship with him to the next level, however I almost never saw this individual again.

I started my junior year towards the end of September. After not working for nearly three months, I arrived at dining services convinced that everything was frozen in time. I spent several days searching for Chris because I planned to catch up. Four weeks passed and I was ominous that he would never return. During this time I became deeply depressed—I was crushed by the thought I would never see him again. For the next seven months I masked this pain because I did not want anyone to know I was hurting inside. I felt extremely empty because I wanted to say "goodbye." Throughout the school year I constantly scanned my environment to see if I would ever see him again.

Throughout college I ran into co-workers, professors, friends, and even teaching assistants at SeaTac International Airport. This facility is the perfect place to reunite with acquaintances because it is the only major airport that serves Puget Sound. Shortly before I left for Winter Break, I arrived four hours before my scheduled departure because I wanted to spend extra time searching for him. Although I scouted the entire airport, he never surfaced.

On April 23, 2012 I was greeted by an unusually clear and sunny sky. Once I stepped outside Smith Hall I received several text messages from my best friend Claire Mueller. Over the past few months, we developed a strong friendship. Two months ago we both teamed up to do a joint speech regarding same-sex marriage. Instead of meeting to discuss political strategies, we reviewed modifications to our department's grading system. Although I was cheerful to see my best friend—I was deeply anxious to unmask a seven-month secret. As I walked across Red Square and witnessed a breathtaking view of Rainer Vista, I realized I had something to smile about.

During this sunny afternoon I met with Claire inside a secluded courtyard. Once we finished our meeting—I revealed the moment I first fell in love. When I was fourteen years old my brain was not fully developed. As a result, I was attracted to men for the wrong reasons because I only saw what stood in front of me. I discussed how undeveloped brains (especially in teenagers) enables the human mind to separate romance and sexual intercourse. This stratification removes two important components to sustaining healthy relationships. As I got older my outlook regarding human attraction broadened. Since moving to a city with the second highest proportion of LGBT residents I've had the pleasure of meeting men I never knew existed.

I revealed to Claire the first time I was attracted to someone others overlooked. During my sophomore year, I experienced a rare ability to detect an individual's beauty beneath the surface. This stranger's inner life was masked behind a reserved exterior. For several months, I tried to break his silence because he put a smile on my face. When I first met this individual I was drawn to discovering his inner life. Behind his eyes and beneath his skin lied someone's child, relative, friend, student, and co-worker. Meeting this person taught me that love doesn't come in a particular race, sex, age, or faith.

The most painful part of this discussion occurred when I stated; "I returned to work believing everything was *frozen in time...*" Shortly after starting my third-year of college I faced a rude awakening. The one person I was looking forward to see was not one of the few surviving relics. This was not a minor miscalculation, but a missed opportunity to take a relationship with someone to the next level. The evaporation of morning dew each day became more evident than ever before. Although I rarely embrace (a mentality of) living my life in present, I learned the importance of using everyday to forge meaningful relationships. I do not know when I will live my final day. As a result, I began to view each day as my last before waking up. I also need to overcome my fear of expressing my feelings to others because I don't know if that is the last time I see them.

Shortly after pouring my heart out—I thanked Claire for her support and gave her a long-lasting hug before going home. My conversation with her helped heal seven months of personal regrets. To this day I remain thankful she was there for me because I began applying the values I learned from our conversation the following day. What gave me the strength to remain in Washington were the incredible people I met along the way. I was very fortunate to enroll in a great major, secure an excellent internship, and know people who believed in me.

A Second Chance

April 24, 2012 was just a normal day on my calendar. With the exception of attending an early meeting at University Heights and completing some homework—I didn't schedule many activities. This meeting with Dorothy Lengyel was shockingly brief (her schedule was booked with several meetings throughout the day). As we rapidly reviewed numerous playground documents and finalized last minute details for an upcoming meeting, I was free to leave. Just before I left the office I wrote down a list of weekly tasks. As I walked through the hallway I briefly thought if I should pay a visit to Katy Buck. Within an instant I realized, "I *must* catch up on school work."

Once I left the premises of University Heights—I was smacked by the presence of someone I lost. As I gazed across a busy street I saw a young white man. This stranger was not only handsome, but his dark brown hair and setback eye sockets *screamed* the identity of a familiar face. For the first few seconds my brain was examining if the individual across the street was in fact my college crush. As I stared at this man, my heart was gushing. I was finally reunited.

The person I searched for nearly seven months was only a few feet away. I lost control of my own body. I felt my stomach succumb to gravity. This moment caught me by complete surprise—I had no clue what my next action was. I didn't prepare any speech or strategize a first date.

There was no time to think. I was forced to act *immediately* because I had to live my life to the fullest. Before I was able to embark on this reunification, four lanes of busy traffic stood in the way. The first decision almost involved *risking* my entire life. I jaywalked across one of Seattle's busiest streets during morning rush hour. If there was one last thing I accomplished before the end of the day it was saying "goodbye." My body came within *just feet* of direct contact with an automobile driving 45 miles per hour.

Just after seeing my life flash before my eyes, I yelled, *"Chris, how are you?"* As I was wheezing for oxygen I did my best to compose myself. I asked him, *"Do you remember me...* worked at dining services. How is your family doing in California?"

Once I revealed my name he remembered me. I was elated to know he never forgot me. My casual conversations during the past year actually paid off. As I walked Chris to his bus stop, he informed me that he accepted a research position at the Fred Hutchinson Cancer Research Center. In addition, he told me that he is going to start pursuing a PhD in Clinical Psychology at Rutgers University.

One question I asked Chris was where he envisioned himself in the next five years. He informed me that he hopes to someday become a psychology professor at a prestigious university. He also mentioned that on his bucket list he wants to pet a panda and invent a flavor of Ben and Jerry's ice cream. I told him my dream is to champion human rights. I expressed how I met the author of Washington's same-sex marriage bill and how I planned to spend the next several months advocating for marriage equality.

Without even a moment's notice, Chris asked a really tough question, "What gave you the strength to move across the country at age 19?" For just a few seconds I stood silent because I was deliberating about whether or not to provide an honest answer. Ultimately, I did not feel comfortable providing an honest answer because I feared his reaction. Instead of stating what was on my mind, I informed him that the University of Washington has the third oldest planning program in the nation.

I did not tell Chris that it was people like him who gave me the strength of will and emotion to venture 3,000 miles outside my comfort zone. I did not feel comfortable telling him that it was not about the place, but what mattered most was the *people* and *experience*. I believed Chris would be more appeased by logical answers. The main reason I did not provide a more altruistic response was that I deeply feared he would walk away.

Although many friends believe I am highly expressive, I experienced great difficulty sustaining this conversation. The reason I struggled was not because I lacked ideas, but I really felt fulfilled. There were times I thought about leaving Chris before his bus arrived, however I waited seven long months to enjoy this precious moment with him.

For the next few minutes I just stared at him like a cheerful teenager during a first date. I did not need to engage in a full conversation because I was simply content with his presence. I was elated that I was able to spend ten minutes with this remarkable person. As I glanced up at Seattle's overcast sky, I entered a brief daze. I was living a dream.

Once his bus pulled over he began walking away. Before he left I shouted, *"Goodbye!"*

Before his bus drove off I started walking back home. I was engulfed in silence for the next several seconds. As soon as his bus faded into the distance, I exclaimed, *"Yes...I did it! I did it! I did it!"* My reunification with Chris made my day because I was beaming with happiness.

Reunification is the most beautiful part of the human experience. Seeing his face (for the first time in nearly seven months) felt better than Christmas. The first person I informed about that amazing morning was Claire Mueller. As I gleefully shared this story, she was proud that I had the strength to not only cross four lanes of busy traffic, but strike up a casual conversation with someone I loved.

April 24, 2012 changed my outlook on how I view human relationships. Although I was never able to ask Chris on a date, I was content to finally receive closure. Before I left Chris, I knew he would live an amazing life. As I closed this chapter with him, it helped me acquire the confidence to approach others. Since that morning I have seized great memories with countless people. I am less fearful today to sacrifice my own comfort because the guilt I repressed was far more painful than the risk of social rejection.

April 24, 2012 marked the final time I encountered Chris. I was really thankful that I received a second chance to say "goodbye." This experience reaffirms the importance of using the past as an instructive opportunity to forge a better tomorrow.

11 NEVER GIVE UP

"Sometimes doors open and others close and you have to figure out which one you're going to take. I'm always for the one that's challenging. That's where I think you live your life to the fullest."
-Gisele Bündchen

On June 16, 2013 I awakened to a piercing sound. At 3:30 am my alarm clock went off. Aside from feeling exhausted (the morning after Graduation), I was reluctant to listen to my alarm because I did not want to leave my home. Early that morning my family and I were scheduled to board a flight to Boston.

It was more difficult for me to get out of bed because I didn't want to leave the Emerald City.

I was the first person in my family to use the shower. As I hopped inside my final shower in Western Washington a million thoughts poured through my head. I was mute because I spent the past three years not only building a strong reputation, but I discovered my own identity throughout this process.

While my family was getting ready, I used this time to savor my final hours. During the past several days I went through all my belongings and cleared my closet. As I was moving out of my house, I came across small gifts and old notes. As I reviewed past memories—I came across a giant piece of paper with several colorful handwritten messages. Just before Graduation, Caitlin Dean taped a giant piece of paper to each student's back and had everyone within our program write a nice comment.

The purpose of this activity was to allow students to knowingly or anonymously say "goodbye." For the longest time I tucked this colorful piece of paper inside a secret space. I did not want to read the comments other students wrote because I wanted to save it for when I felt sad.

During that morning, I finally opened up this piece of paper. As I read this document I was submerged with great memories. One student wrote, "You have continued to surprise me with your enthusiasm and motivation. Keep on doing great work and making people smile." Another message from Adam read, "You are an *amazing* organizer with amazing passion!" The best one came from Claire when she wrote, "You're inspiring and bring energy to *every* room you enter. Never stop being you!" As I finished reading this beautiful document, I neatly tucked it inside my backpack. I carried that special piece of paper on my back because it helped me through this day.

Just before I left the hotel, I carefully searched through my bags because I did not want to forget anything. The night before, my mother and I spent several hours closing shop. A few minutes before my family was ready to leave, I carefully examined our room one last time to make sure nothing was left behind. These final minutes strained my attention span because I couldn't ignore the thought of leaving my favorite place.

Just after closing the door, I ran several feet to catch up with my father. As I was walking through a calmly lit hallway, I was carrying my most precious memories and emotions. I was a delicate piece of china speeding towards a brick wall.

At 4:37 am I stepped outside—I was covered in complete darkness. Even though the sun was already shining over my future, I was walking through an expansive mystery. During this moment there were no immediate opportunities or future plans. I had no clue what would conspire over the next several days or even months. The future had yet to be written. Before I finished college I did not secure employment or nail down where I would be in the next five years.

As my family finished packing our rental van I only recall raw emotions. I was not sure how I should feel. Although I was happy to overcome autism and finish college, I felt sour over the fact I was returning to Connecticut. During the past several minutes I asked myself, "Am I a loser for moving back to Connecticut?" For several moments I wondered if I let down an important promise I made when I was thirteen years old. Did I really stay true to my word by returning to Connecticut—if I fought so hard, *why* was I going back?

During the early hours my body slithered through a tightly packed van. Just before I last stepped foot in Washington, I spent a few seconds enjoying a final view of the Cascade Mountains. My father parked outside a deserted gas station. This area encompassed breathtaking views of Western Washington. Shortly after I tumbled onto solid asphalt, I was greeted with twilight. After being engulfed in darkness for the past several hours, the sun was rising over Puget Sound.

A pink sky radiated across my entire body. I witnessed orange rays of energy invade an unlit atmosphere. The sky's transition from ebony to orange illuminated a purple backdrop against the Cascade Mountains. A mountain range historically dark green remained purple for several minutes. Expansive shadows silhouetted countless Evergreens against a beautiful vista. This view resembled something found inside an artist's imagination, for just a few minutes I left reality behind and embraced my final twilight as a Washingtonian.

Just before I left the Talaris Conference Center my father grabbed one last copy of the *Seattle Times* to read on our flight to Boston. As I cleared through my final security screening at SeaTac International Airport, I recalled the moment I first stepped foot inside this facility.

Three years ago I left a small town where I spent the first nineteen years of my life. I moved because my life was not good enough. I wanted to live somewhere that allowed me to evolve into a stronger person. Stepping 3,000 miles outside of my comfort zone was crucial to solidifying my identity and values. I never envisioned that I would ever have the opportunity to help advance same-sex marriage and reach out to the former President of South Africa.

Living in the Emerald City reassured that I was not an ugly duckling. Over the past three years I was able to share personal stories with countless individuals and forge new friendships. The hardest part about June 16, 2013 was leaving behind several friends.

Shortly after 6:00 am my best friend Claire Mueller sent a text message, "Bye Gabe! I'll miss you!" Once I received her message I smiled. Although I was happy to know she was thinking of me, reading her message made it more difficult to mask the pain I felt. For the next several minutes I looked outside the terminal to enjoy my final minutes in Washington. I did my best to turn my eye away from the future and only focus on the present.

Before the thought "of here and now" crossed my mind an airline worker called our flight for Boston. Just before Zone 3 was announced, Claire sent a final text,

> *"You're wonderful Gabe.* Be happy because we got to spend two amazing years together, and we will spend many more e-mailing, visiting, and otherwise being friends."

As I walked to my assigned seat (located along the back row) I thought about what Claire expressed. I should feel jubilant to reside on the East Coast because it's home to many excellent graduate programs. In addition, I possess a stronger platform to advance the rights of gays and lesbians. Moving 3,000 miles away from my comfort zone (this time around) allowed me to not only enjoy a better selection of planning programs, but I encountered another unique opportunity to continue my fight for humanity.

Once the plane pushed away from the gate I tried to maintain a straight face. As the plane came closer to the third runway, it became more and more difficult to control my emotions. I could no longer hide my true feelings. As I heard an explosive sound emerge from the plane's wings reality finally sunk in. I closed my eyes for just a second and tried to think positively. I used my hat as a mask to hide my face. As soon as I felt my body pull against gravity a waterfall rolled down my face for the next forty minutes.

Windsor v. United States

Shortly after returning to Connecticut the United States Supreme Court struck down Section 3 of the Defense of Marriage Act in *Windsor v. United States*. June 26, 2013 was a historic day for the gay rights movement because the United States Supreme Court affirmed that the federal government could not disavow states that already recognized same-sex marriage. Same-sex couples who married in states that already passed same-sex marriage such as Connecticut and Washington would have their marriage recognized by the federal government. This meant that married same-sex couples would be able to jointly file taxes, collect the Social Security benefits of a deceased spouse, and have inheritance rights.

Despite the fact that part of the Defense of Marriage Act was overturned, I was really disappointed at the Supreme Court for not going far enough. The United States Supreme Court was craven for not addressing the *Hollingsworth v. Perry* case. In June 2013 only thirteen states permitted same-sex marriage. As a result, most Americans did not immediately benefit because the high court failed to address the recognition of same-sex marriage across state lines. In addition, the court never mentioned what would happen if states were to rollback same-sex marriage.

Whenever same-sex marriage reached a high court, many countries confronted it including Brazil and South Africa. The justices on those courts did not *duck* certain cases because they feared political backlash. I was more upset that a country once ruled under Apartheid was surpassing the United States when it came to human rights. I could not believe the Constitutional Court of South Africa had more courage than the United States Supreme Court to uphold same-sex marriage.

On November 30, 2006 South Africa became the fifth country in the world to legalize same-sex marriage. In *Minister of Home Affairs v. Fourie* the Constitutional Court of South Africa ruled 8-1 that Parliament must enact same-sex marriage legislation within twelve months. Justice Kate O'Reagan was the lone dissent in the *Minister of Home Affairs v. Fourie* case. In her opinion she stated that the *court* should write the same-sex marriage ruling into law (not the legislature):

> "The doctrine of the separation of powers is an important one in our Constitution but I cannot see that it can be used to avoid the obligation of a court to provide *appropriate relief* that is just and equitable to litigants who successfully raise a constitutional complaint."

Had Justice O'Reagan served on the United States Supreme Court during the *Hollingsworth v. Perry* case there would be a different outcome. The three branches of government each have distinct responsibilities. It is the solemn obligation of courts to protect the rights of minorities. Justice O'Reagan was the *only* member of the Constitutional Court who fulfilled her promise to defending the Constitution of South Africa. She believed that politically powerless groups could *not* advance the change that was needed to improve their well-being.

Another purpose of the judiciary system is (to issue rulings which are designed) to add additional layers of constitutional safeguards that prevent people from having their rights eliminated. States that legalized same-sex marriage through legislative statue do not have the same safeguards as those with a ruling from a state supreme court. The only way to overturn a court ruling in Connecticut is to amend the constitution. Amending the Connecticut Constitution is an exhaustive process because it requires a supermajority vote in the legislature and it has to undergo a statewide referendum. States that enacted same-sex marriage through the legislative process can repeal a law once lawmakers secured a simple majority. Shortly after the Republican Party took control of the New Hampshire General Court in 2011, they held a vote to repeal the state's same-sex marriage law (which passed in 2009).

Since the high court declined to issue a universal ruling for same-sex marriage, they did not resolve the legal inconsistencies people face on a daily basis. As courts step back, the welfare of the LGBT community hangs at the mercy of the existing political leadership in government. When countries grant extensive political autonomy to states using a federation style of governance there are going to be considerable disparities resulting from varied laws. For instance, the United States Supreme Court failed to explain what would occur if a legally married same-sex couple moved to a state that did not recognize private contracts between same-sex couples. According to the Marshall-Newman Amendment, private contracts between same-sex couples are not recognized under Virginia's Constitution. This provision revokes a person's medical power of attorney (even if they are legally married in another state).

Justice O'Reagan raised an important question. If courts are not going to extend justice, equality, or human dignity to marginalized communities; who would advocate on behalf of those in society that are most vulnerable to oppression?

I was determined to keep fighting for others because I could not afford to stop during this critical moment. At the end of the day the struggle continues. What happened in Connecticut and Washington was crucial because it sent a message to the federal government that same-sex marriage *will not* disappear. As more states legalized same-sex marriage I knew this would become a national issue. In two or three years, the United States Supreme Court would likely revisit this issue once and for all.

Applying to Graduate School

Since my sophomore year of high school I knew I needed to attain a graduate degree in order to become an urban planner. I researched over twenty graduate programs across eighteen states. Although I was deeply impressed at the graduate program at the University of Washington—I could not afford to pay out-of-state tuition for another two years. In addition, their planning department stressed design over policy. I was apprehensive that having a strong background in politics would alienate me from fellow students.

Since April 2008 I have dreamed of living in New York City (which is home to four accredited urban planning programs). Although I did not intend on applying to Columbia or New York University this time around, my sights were set on Hunter College and Rutgers University. My favorite aspect about Rutgers was that it bridged public policy and city planning. Another guilty reason I wanted to attend Rutgers was the fact Chris was pursuing his doctoral degree on campus. During my senior year of college I joked frequently about how I would plan "secret outings" to his office hours. In addition, I strategized one plan—which involved getting lost in the School of Psychology and magically re-appearing during his office hours. Like many young people, I fantasized about love. In fact, I still wanted to shower this person with small gifts.

On December 16, 2013 I received my first acceptance from Ohio State University. The Master of City and Regional Planning (MCRP) program is flexible because it allows students to customize their planning concentration. In addition, this program was already equipped with a solid internship database. Moving to Ohio assured me great employment opportunities.

On February 18, 2014 I was accepted into the University of California, Irvine. I was amazed to be admitted into the nation's top public university system. Although the University of California, Irvine was a great school, their planning program lacked substance. I was disappointed at the high number of restricted electives students were forced to take. In addition, the program did not offer courses that matched my interests.

By early April I received rejection notices from both Rutgers University and Hunter College. My rejection from Rutgers University caught me by surprise because their program has a large enrollment (which usually means more students are admitted during each application cycle). I couldn't understand why Rutgers would turn down someone who graduated from the University of Washington.

Although Rutgers was my top choice, I realized that I wanted to enroll for the wrong reasons. I needed to step outside my comfort zone once again.

Before I applied to colleges, my high school guidance counselor told me that as a student from Connecticut I had a better chance being admitted into schools on the West Coast. The reason I enjoyed a greater chance being admitted into the University of Washington (instead of New York University) was because most applicants were from a four-hour radius. By applying to schools where a majority of applicants are from a different region—I was able to distinguish myself. Great things do not come easy and sometimes I need to sacrifice my own comfort in order to evolve into a better individual.

My comfort zone correlates to environments that fostered full equality for gays and lesbians. I wanted to live in New York since I was seventeen years old because it was only a handful of jurisdictions that recognized same-sex marriage. My comfort zone stretched across the Northeast because it was the only region that embraced marriage equality.

By 2013 the number of states that passed same-sex marriage increased to thirteen. If I wanted to marry somebody—I wasn't forced to live someplace buried beneath two feet of snow. Furthermore, it was nice to know I could live in warmer climates. At that moment I realized moving to New York City was just a great fallacy because my needs emerged in more places overtime. Since I was young, I've always *fixated* on living in a specific *place*. As I got older, I realized that it's not about the place, what matters most are the *people* and *experience*. Had I spent my entire life in places where I enjoyed full rights—I would never have any opportunities to fight for others.

After being denied by Rutgers University and Hunter College my decision came down to Ohio State University or University of California, Irvine. A hard choice stood directly in front of me because I wasn't sure whether or not I would remain inside my comfort zone. Although I really wanted to move back to the West Coast, Ohio State's graduate program was more in line with my interests. In my acceptance letter from Ohio State I was offered a paid internship. Despite this lucrative opportunity, I was ready for palm trees and Pacific breeze.

12 LIVING UNDER A GLASS CEILING

"Although we were not able to shatter that highest glass ceiling this time, thanks to you it has 18 million cracks in it..."
-Hillary Rodham Clinton

A giant glass ceiling stretches between the Ohio River and Lake Erie. On August 20, 2014 I entered Ohio's glass ceiling to start a new chapter. I was beginning my graduate studies at Ohio State University. I decided to enroll in their Master of City and Regional Planning program since I wasn't accepted anywhere East.

For much of my adult life I resided in an environment that theoretically ensured equality for LGBT citizens. My home state was not only the second state to legalize same-sex marriage, but it was the second state to enact hate crime legislation. In 1989 Connecticut approved legislation granting equal access to IVF for all couples and individuals. I was going from a place where I enjoyed all my rights—to some place where everything I took for granted would quickly *vanish*.

The biggest misgiving about attending Ohio State was residing in a place with such a conservative history. In 2004 Ohio voters approved Issue 1, which not only outlawed same-sex marriage, but prohibited civil unions from being recognized under the state's constitution. This policy barred gays and lesbians from receiving several rights. The *cruelest* part of this provision was the state's constitution precluded same-sex couples from receiving funeral arrangements and hospital visitations. In addition, twenty-seven domestic violence criminals were wrongfully released from state prisons because Ohio refused to recognize *any* legal contracts between unmarried couples. After three years of legal chaos, an Ohio court finally reversed those overturned convictions.

The most *deplorable* aspect of Ohio's glass ceiling is the hostility state government holds towards the transgender community. In 1987 an Ohio court ruled state law does not allow anyone to amend the sex information listed on an individual's birth certificate (even after an individual completes a sex reassignment surgery). Since the *In Re: Declaratory Relief For Ladrach* ruling was issued, courts have determined that transgender individuals are not able to legally marry anyone of the opposite sex because a sex change doesn't constitute as being a legal error on an Ohio birth certificate.

When I first discovered Ohio was one of three states that don't issue new birth certificates to individuals who undergo a sex reassignment surgery—I was appalled. I had to go to Columbus to *stop* the political assault against the LGBT community. Even though I was deeply anxious about moving to a place where I enjoyed fewer rights, I heard another call to go forth into the world because I knew my fight for human dignity was not over. I was *determined* to continue sharing my story. Although I never planned to live beneath a glass ceiling, I realized I had a job to finish.

Another Anti-Bullying Law

Before I arrived in Columbus, I scheduled a meeting with State Representative Michael Stinziano. Earlier he introduced anti-bullying legislation in Ohio. I decided to reach out to him because I believed that I could apply my legislative experience to help advance this important cause. During my graduate orientation I made a secret outing to Representative Stinziano's office because I wanted to share my ideas to improving the quality-of-life for LGBT residents across Ohio.

On August 26, 2014 I met with Representative Stinziano for over an hour. He and I both discussed legislative strategies and covered each step to passing legislation. Republicans not only dominate both chambers of the Ohio General Assembly, but they control each of the legislative committees. Since Democrats are in the minority, Stinziano enjoyed fewer opportunities to hold legislative hearings because those events are scheduled at the discretion of each committee Chair.

Stinziano mentioned that the Chairs of both the Judiciary and Education committee *opposed* previous efforts to protecting gays and lesbians from discrimination. The reason passing this bill was so difficult was that it required approval in both committees before undergoing a final vote in front of the entire legislative chamber.

Another roadblock this bill experienced was the fact Ohio's largest gay rights organization opposed protecting gays and lesbians from violence in public schools. Equality Ohio issued a statement *urging* Representative Stinziano to *not* introduce any anti-bullying legislation during the current legislative session. Despite the rampant occurrence of teen suicides across the country, Equality Ohio was more focused on pursuing other legislative activities. I was extremely disheartened to learn that an organization intended on protecting the rights of gay, lesbian, and transgender residents across Ohio was not fulfilling its own mission.

Before I left Stinziano's office he advised me to contact Representative Tim Brown who is an openly gay Republican. Stinziano ultimately believed there were better prospects introducing this legislation with a Republican colleague. Although Representative Brown previously supported anti-bullying legislation in Ohio, I was warned that Brown would be reluctant to introduce such legislation in fear of political retaliation from his own party.

I felt discouraged as I walked outside the Riffe Center because I was against many significant forces. Once I arrived home I wrote a letter to Representative Brown. I used this opportunity to explain *why* Ohio needs to protect LGBT students from discrimination. Furthermore, I revealed how HB 74 (the current legislative proposal) is farce because it fails to specify the real victims of school violence. I did my best to *urge* Representative Brown to lead this fight because countless students in Ohio want to feel safe in their community. I not only offered my support for this legislation, but I expressed deep interest testifying in favor of this issue.

On October 15, 2014 Representative Brown notified me that HB 74 passed the Ohio House of Representatives last year. Although this provision prohibited "bullying" in public schools, it disregards incorporating enumerated categories such as sexual orientation and gender identity. This provision was farce because the language was too vague. Even if HB 74 were signed, school districts across Ohio would not receive enough clarity to properly address bullying and discrimination.

Representative Brown mentioned that including enumerated categories required the entire legislative process to start from scratch. He directed me to Representative Marlene Anielski (who authored HB 74). She designed HB 74 so that sexual orientation and gender identity *would not* be considered a protected-class under Ohio law. Instead of using his position in state government to rectify this critical issue, Representative Brown sold his political integrity in order to position himself for a lucrative leadership position within the Republican Party. His decision to ignore the welfare of countless students across Ohio demonstrates his thirst for political gain. As I finished reading his message I became *disgusted* at how permissive he was allowing the Republican Party to derail any progress of gay rights.

HB 74 was never voted by the State Senate and died at the end of the year. The reason this bill failed was the fact too many leaders feared making hard choices. When the School Violence Prevention Act passed in North Carolina there was a strong appetite from students, state lawmakers, school administrators, labor unions, and teachers. The issue of school violence became such a serious issue that it was impossible for state officials to ignore. North Carolina was fortunate to have compassionate people organize a meaningful solution. Throughout the legislative session, numerous professionals within North Carolina's education community testified in favor of the School Violence Prevention Act.

My experience in Ohio reminds me of the political obstacles I would have likely faced had I lobbied for gay rights in Florida or Virginia—Republicans *will* obstruct gay rights without any remorse.

Although acceptance for gay rights is rising, it's rare for states to voluntarily adopt reforms to prevent discrimination. When I first entered politics I knew before I started to advocate for legislation that I needed to campaign in a state equipped with a Democratic legislature. Unlike Ohio, the Democratic Party historically controlled North Carolina politics. As a result, many politicians in North Carolina understood the needs of the gay community. Many members of the legislature became sympathetic of my story and the hardships I faced growing up.

Perseverance is key to overcoming any obstacle. Steve Jobs made a famous statement, "Sometimes life's going to hit you in the head with a brick. Don't lose faith. I'm convinced that the only thing that kept me going was that I loved what I did." If my life were a fairy tale—I would never acquire the strength of will or emotion to take on serious challenges. If everything were perfect—I would not become the compassionate person I am today.

Although I was disappointed at state lawmakers, securing any political victory is no easy task. I am fully comfortable knowing I will face failures in my career, however I *refuse* to be defined by past mistakes. Since I was young I have used my past experience as an instructive opportunity to strive towards a better tomorrow. Regardless of this legislative outcome, my dignity and determination will never fade.

Proud Feminist: Gay Rights Speech in Ohio

The next opportunity I had to shatter Ohio's glass ceiling occurred on October 28, 2014. During that morning my class discussed issues related to feminism, gender, and sexual orientation. Prior to class I was unusually quiet. I spent the previous night ensuring that I prepared a robust speech. I even went to great lengths lining up oral arguments and researching important data. If I could touch one person—I accomplished my objective.

By the start of class my stomach was churning. My professor Bernadette Hanlon asked students to raise their hand if they considered themself a feminist (I was the only man to do so). Students laughed once I raised my hand. Although I alienated myself from my own colleagues—I had to self-identify as a feminist because there is a special political coalition between women's rights and gay rights.

The most significant issue that unites women and the LGBT community is the Equal Rights Amendment. Since 1972 thirty-five states have ratified the Equal Rights Amendment. In 1974 Connecticut voters approved an amendment barring sex discrimination in the state constitution. Since this measure passed, courts have extended protections of this amendment to include sexual orientation and gender identity.

Having an Equal Rights Amendment embedded in a state constitution is critical to ensuring that marriage rights are extended to same-sex couples. Courts in Massachusetts, Iowa, Connecticut, and California determined that denying a marriage license to a lesbian couple *is* sex discrimination. Although Congress never ratified the Equal Rights Amendment, this proposal has not only helped women, but it has advanced the rights of the LGBT community.

The first half of class was brutal because it only covered gender issues. The eternal discussion of gender prolonged my anxiety because I was dying to open up about how difficult it is for homosexuals to live in Ohio. As the clock kept ticking my nerves increased. As my anxiety continued to rise I did not think I would ever speak. One girl in class said, "We'll *never* get to *your* topic given the current place…"

As I waited patiently to speak with my right hand raised—my written arguments were ready. I was determined to make a *powerful* statement. I had been quiet for too long and it was time for me to break my silence. By this time my heart was racing and I was afraid that I would humiliate myself. My adrenaline was setting in and I was ready to transform into my own champion. Without a moment's notice, Bernadette called my name and the floor was mine.

> "In 2004 voters in Ohio passed Issue 1 which outlawed same-sex marriage and civil unions. Since then courts have not allowed same-sex couples to jointly adopt. In addition, the legislature has never addressed the issue of hate crimes. What is most cruel is that Ohio is one of three states where individuals who undergo a sex reassignment surgery are not issued a new birth certificate. In this state I do not have any rights to hospital visitation, burial rights, and I do not have legal authority to investigate a wrong death claim if my partner were to die. I also do not have testimonial privileges in Ohio courts. What's even worse is that if my partner becomes sick I will not be eligible for sick leave because the federal government does not recognize civil unions or domestic partnerships.

> Ohio's discrimination against LGBT individuals comes at a great cost. Between 1993-2008 231,000 taxpayers have left Ohio. According to the Tax Foundation, Ohio has lost $19 billion of Adjusted Gross Income during that time period.

> People's rights should not end at the city limit. We

> need to extend people's rights across state lines. As planners we should make sure that cities are taking adequate measures to embrace diversity and social equity. Our state should work to expand equality and human dignity. What I have seen come out of the Ohio legislature is *hurtful* and *must* be stopped. People are being *deprived* their citizenship on daily basis."

As soon as I finished my speech the class was silent. My heart sank. Just after giving an impassioned speech I quickly acted as if nothing happened. I was waiting for critical comments, however I stunned my colleagues.

Following my speech one student lauded me for what I said and agreed that public policy *is* essential to creating inclusive communities. At least two students asked me if human migration is directly related to oppressive legislation.

In urban planning there is often a human element that is left out. I did my best to shed light on the fact people in Ohio are being *oppressed* on a daily basis. Furthermore, I expressed how *hurtful* it is to not have access to federal or state marriage benefits. My objective was to send a powerful message—it's really *painful* to be deprived hospital visitations and funeral arrangements. The LGBT community faces tremendous obstacles. As a result, I used my position as a graduate student to illustrate the challenges I (and other gay men) encounter each day.

Once somebody speaks out on issues that directly impact them, it's easier for others to acquire a unique perspective on what challenges a marginalized citizen in society must face. At the end of the day, I hope more people will question our laws and aspire for better policies. People need to be reminded that public policy *does matter* and that it's crucial for government to represent your interests.

Sixth Circuit: Separation of Powers Nonexistent

On November 6, 2014 the United States Court of Appeals for the Sixth Circuit upheld same-sex marriage bans in four states (including Ohio). A district panel of three judges concluded that states *have* the legal authority to limit marriage to opposite-sex couples.

Two of the judges assigned to this case were Republican appointees. In *DeBoer v. Snyder* the Sixth Circuit Court of Appeals ruled 2-1 the United States Constitution is *not* a living document. Judge Jeffrey Sutton and Judge Deborah Cook determined that the Constitution was not designed to permit same-sex marriage:

> "Federal judges engaged in the inherent pacing that comes with living constitutionalism should appreciate the inherent pacing that comes with democratic majorities deciding within reasonable bounds when and whether to embrace an evolving, as opposed to settled, societal norm."

This ruling sharply contrasts *Kerrigan v. Commissioner of Public Health* because the Connecticut Supreme Court revealed that constitutions serve as a "living document." Connecticut's highest court noted the importance of having judges not interpret a constitution "too narrowly." The Sixth Circuit issued a ruling, which refrains from addressing a serious constitutional question. In addition, the Sixth Circuit panel expressed that the issue of same-sex marriage is determined by the legislative *not* judiciary branch of government:

> "Isn't the goal to create a culture in which a majority of citizens dignify and respect the rights of minority groups through majoritarian laws rather than through decisions issued by a majority of Supreme Court Justices? It is dangerous and demeaning to the citizenry to assume that *we*, and only *we*, can fairly understand the arguments for and against gay marriage."

Despite the fact gays and lesbians are discriminated on a daily basis, the Sixth Circuit Court of Appeals believed that voters have the authority to prevent same-sex couples from getting married. This decision not only reinforces the glass ceiling Ohio is under, but it reiterates the fear Justice O'Reagan articulated in her dissent in *Minister of Home Affairs v. Fourie*. Justice O'Reagan condemned high courts for turning over judiciary responsibilities to the legislative branch of government. The decision by the Sixth Circuit illustrates that courts are reluctant to rectify issues in front of them. The purpose of judicial systems is to clarify and interpret laws so they are aligned in a consistent manner. The Sixth Circuit Court of

Appeals justified inconsistency—they found it permissible to discriminate against gays and lesbians across state lines.

The Sixth Circuit Court of Appeals is the *least* influential federal court system in the country. According to the *SCOTUS Blog*, decisions issued by the Sixth Circuit were reversed by the United States Supreme Court 24 out of the 25 times they were reviewed in the five annual terms starting in October 2008 and ending in June 2013—a higher frequency than any other federal appellate court during that time period. I knew the Sixth Circuit's authority was questionable (even before they heard the same-sex marriage case). Since decisions from this district are typically out of step—I had an optimistic feeling this case would in fact propel same-sex marriage to the United States Supreme Court.

EPILOGUE

"Too many of us have been standing around waiting for things to happen instead of making things happen."
-Leanne Manas

On June 26, 2015 the United States Supreme Court issued a landmark decision paving the way for same-sex marriage nationwide in *Obergefell v. Hodges*. The Supreme Court ruled 5-4 that gay marriage bans in Ohio, Tennessee, Michigan, and Kentucky violated the United States Constitution. The justices acknowledged that states *must* issue marriage licenses and recognize same-sex marriages legally performed in another jurisdiction. This ruling is a tremendous victory for the gay rights movement because it resolves years of legal ambiguity.

Same-sex marriage would not be possible for the entire country if it was not for the four justices on the Connecticut Supreme Court who determined the state's statutory ban was unconstitutional. Several years after the *Kerrigan v. Commissioner of Public Health* decision, I reached out to former Connecticut Supreme Court Justice Joette Katz. I thanked Justice Katz for joining the majority opinion. I also explained how the *Kerrigan v. Commissioner of Public Health* ruling empowered me to fight for the rights of politically powerless groups. In addition, I informed her that I championed a comprehensive anti-bullying law in North Carolina.

When I first testified in front of the North Carolina legislature only eight states shielded students from discrimination. By the end of 2014 nineteen states approved legislation, which adequately protects LGBT students from bullying. Following the passage of the School Violence Prevention Act, Republicans took control of the North Carolina legislature. Despite the change in leadership, this law was never repealed. In fact, legislation was passed in 2011 to strengthen this law by adding cyberbullying to North Carolina's anti-bullying statue.

On the six-year anniversary of the *Kerrigan v. Commissioner of Public Health* ruling, a federal judge lifted North Carolina's ban on same-sex marriage. On October 10, 2014 North Carolina became the second southern state to permit gay marriage. There is no question the School Violence Prevention Act positioned North Carolina to legalize same-sex marriage. Passing gay rights legislation paved the way for North Carolina's LGBT community to receive justice. In addition, it was crucial to campaign early because I was *determined* to ensure this state moved towards promoting equal rights.

Although there are some benefits to advancing the rights of gays and lesbians through the legislative branch of government, same-sex marriage had to ultimately be decided by the courts. As I mentioned earlier: "the primary purpose of the judiciary system is to issue rulings which are designed to add additional layers of constitutional safeguards that prevent people from having their rights eliminated." Unlike a judicial ruling, countries that legalized same-sex marriage through the legislative process do not have as many legal safeguards. For example, if Congress passed legislation creating gender-neutral marriage laws, there is nothing that could prevent the next Congress from repealing such policy. Once Republicans won control of the New Hampshire General Court, they held a vote to repeal the state's same-sex marriage law (which Democrats adopted). Despite early actions of well-intended lawmakers—legislative statues are not as resilient as court decisions.

Since the Supreme Court legalized same-sex marriage, the only way to reverse this decision is to amend the United States Constitution. Amending the Constitution is a very rigorous process. Previous attempts to outlaw same-sex marriage in the Constitution have failed. Shortly after Massachusetts legalized same-sex marriage, Republicans introduced the Federal Marriage Amendment.

During the Bush Administration, conservatives tried to prevent states from recognizing gay marriage. Although President Bush urged Congress to approve this provision, his agenda was never met with success. Despite the fact thirty-one states outlawed gay marriage (in their state constitution), supporters of the Federal Marriage Amendment failed to convince enough lawmakers and states to pursue this issue. By the end of 2013 seventeen states permitted same-sex marriage. Once gay rights activists secured enough legislative and judicial victories, the Federal Marriage Amendment eventually became extinguished.

Courts were forced to settle many civil rights issues because lawmakers were on the wrong side of history. For example, many state legislatures across America denied women the opportunity to vote, prohibited interracial marriage, and embraced racial segregation in public schools. Courts must address same-sex marriage because this is the civil rights issue of my generation. In addition, sexual relationships should never be sandwiched in politics. Many gay men including myself never wanted lawmakers to dictate *how* we pull down our underwear.

A New Chapter

Although the United States legalized same-sex marriage, more work must be done. As I reflect on the opportunities and tragedies during these past seven years, I still wonder, "How is the United States a decade behind a country once ruled under Apartheid?" South Africa not only overcame decades of oppression, but it furthered human rights using three crucial ingredients: public policy, leadership, and human imagination. United States Supreme Court Justice Ruth Bader Ginsburg called South Africa's Constitution a major success:

> "I would not look to the United States, if I were drafting a constitution. I might look at the Constitution of South Africa. That was a deliberate attempt to have a fundamental instrument of government that embraced basic human rights, had an independent judiciary...It really is, I think, a great piece of work that

was done. Why not take advantage of what there is elsewhere in the world?"

Justice Ginsburg asked a very serious question, *"Why not take advantage of what there is elsewhere in the world?"* If a Justice serving on the Supreme Court believes the United States is not equipped with the best constitution, my objective is to identify places that exemplify gay rights in their constitution and statues. During the next several years I plan to travel across the world. I intend to benchmark and research best practices regarding human rights.

Going forward, the LGBT community must develop strategies to advance their interests around the world. During my second book I will examine: corrupt governments, flawed democracies, uncodified constitutions, emerging economies, and decades of human oppression. I am going to reveal how gays and lesbians can reside in countries where they enjoy full equality despite significant barriers. In addition, I plan to illustrate why countries are not chained to past mistakes. I will continue where I left off because I have not finished writing. During the next several years I intend to work on human rights because I want to share the journey other countries experienced as they deliver landmark judicial and legislative victories to the LGBT community.

Last Word

Breaking deeply embedded social constructs is no easy task. I was extremely fortunate to work with such a compassionate and supportive group of individuals throughout my career. Changing history *requires* a vivid imagination because great ideas do not stem from reality. Overcoming legislative barriers requires people to come together.

One lesson I learned from writing my first book is that humans *want* to feel belonged wherever they are. This desire has prevented too many people from ever stepping outside their comfort zone. Many people go to great lengths just to acquire social acceptance. Throughout my life I have witnessed progressives and conservatives congregate in communities, schools, and employers where others share their beliefs. This homogenization has caused the nation's society and politics to become more polarized than ever before.

Moving to Ohio was not an easy choice. I personally want to share that I *dreaded* the moment I drove beneath a giant glass ceiling. As a gay man, I felt *dehumanized* to live in place where my rights were practically nonexistent. Despite this difficulty, moving to a conservative area has allowed me to interact with people I would never meet. Stepping outside my comfort zone has added a unique perspective to my personal and professional development because it allowed me to grow. The failure of anti-bullying legislation in Ohio empowered me to continue speaking out on current issues. As a result, I embarked on this project because I want to share my journey with a larger audience.

As I finish writing my first book I want to stress *your* voice truly matters. I strongly encourage you to find an interest or cause that impassions your spirit. Progress will never happen if people remain on the sidelines. I never envisioned a career in politics, however I had no choice but to become political because my rights were almost stripped away by people who never knew me. The first time I believed in miracles and dreams was after I read a state supreme court decision in my home state—at that moment I realized I didn't need a prestigious job title or law degree to make a positive difference. I truly hope reading my story inspires you. I hope this empowers you to become *your* own champion and believe in what's possible.

ACKNOWLEDGEMENTS

I first want to acknowledge and dedicate this book to my grandfather, Charles Filer. You have given me the strength of will and emotion to fight for a person's right to self-determination. You are such an amazing individual. I hope you are proud of my accomplishments. *Always* know you are truly missed.

I really want to thank my family: Daniel Filer, Luanne Filer, and Danielle Filer for their support over the past several years. *Thanks* for allowing me to spend countless holidays writing this book; I hope I've not let you down.

Writing a book is truly a collaborative effort. I am so gratified that I had the opportunity to work with so many incredible people. I want to take this time to specifically thank: Chardon Murray, Claire Mueller, Adam Fahlstrom, Allison Hamburg, Dorothy Lengyel, Ben Weisgal, Mila Limson, Christine Campasano, Christine Wenzel, Melissa Warrek, Rachel Margolis, Caitlin Dean, Chris Campbell, Eddie Plana, Vicky Diaz, Melissa Perez, Emily Janes, Tucker Janes, Amy Smith, Ronnie Rubin, Bonnie Sloan, Cathy Jones, Jamie Pagliaro, Jeanne Kagan, Karen Anthony, Marianne DiStefano, Nicole Charles, Tish Lopez, Sabrina Ryan, Katie Swidarski, Davar Sarbandi, Bernadette Hanlon, Kyle Ezell, Stacia Worndle, Sarah Showalter, Kelly Hostetler, Dana Shukovsky, Lynn Thomas, Catherine Wright, Linda Beloin, and Jennifer DiStefano. At one time *each* of you took a chance on me during my life. I can't thank you enough for believing in me and seeing the potential I had to make this world a better place. *You* are such a wonderful group of people and each of you has a special place in my heart.

ABOUT THE AUTHOR

When I was seventeen years old I started my career as a gay rights activist. During my senior year of high school, I fought against attempts to outlaw same-sex marriage in the Connecticut Constitution. In less than a month, I reached out to over sixty lawmakers and organizations and began advocating for gay rights nationwide. Before I could even vote, I formulated legislative strategies and even used my guidance counselor's office as a phone banking center. I used my study halls to protest politicians for obstructing gay rights. In addition, I teamed with North Carolina State Senator Julia Boseman to help champion the School Violence Prevention Act.

In 2010 I enrolled at the University of Washington. Although I originally intended to become a city planner, I unexpectedly heard another call to re-enter politics. During college I advocated for same-sex marriage. In addition, I worked on several grassroots campaigns. Throughout college I remained politically active. Just before graduation I launched a political blog. In addition, I started working as a freelance journalist. During my tenure, I covered national elections in Australia and South Africa.

In 2013 I graduated from the Community, Environment, and Planning program at the University of Washington. Once I finished college I began pursuing a Master of City and Regional Planning at Ohio State University. During my tenure, I campaigned for anti-bullying legislation in Ohio. My dedication to advancing the rights of gays and lesbians is evident by my record of activism. During my spare time I enjoy writing, traveling, swimming, photography, drafting landscape sketches, and cooking.